CONCISE COLLEGE TEXTS
LAND LAW

OTHER BOOKS IN THE SERIES ARE:

AUSTRALIA
The Law Book Company Ltd.
Sydney : Melbourne : Brisbane

CANADA AND U.S.A.
The Carswell Company Ltd.
Agincourt, Ontario

INDIA
N. M. Tripathi Private Ltd.
Bombay

ISRAEL
Steimatzky's Agency Ltd.
Jerusalem : Tel Aviv : Haifa

MALAYSIA—SINGAPORE—BRUNEI
Malayan Law Journal (Pte) Ltd.
Singapore

NEW ZEALAND
Sweet & Maxwell (N.Z.) Ld.
Wellington

PAKISTAN
Pakistan Law House
Karachi

CONCISE COLLEGE TEXTS

LAND LAW

by

E. SWINFEN GREEN

of Lincoln's Inn, Barrister,
formerly a member of the Board of Management
of the College of Law

THIRD EDITION

by

N. HENDERSON, B.A.

of Middle Temple, Barrister,
a member of the Board of Management
of the College of Law

London
SWEET & MAXWELL
1975

Published in 1975 by
Sweet & Maxwell Limited of
11 New Fetter Lane, London
and
printed in Great Britain by
The Eastern Press Ltd. of
London and Reading

SBN Paperback 421   20110   x
    Hardback   421   20100   2

PREFACE

Most of the changes in this new edition were necessitated by an unusually large number of important decisions affecting the land law, but the opportunity has also been taken to modify the chapter on Settlements and to expand the section on Registration of Title, in recognition of the greater emphasis now placed upon these topics in the Bar Part I (Law of Land) and Part II (Conveyancing) examinations. The Rent Act 1974 came too late to be incorporated fully in the section on Security of Tenure, but its main provisions have been summarised in an Appendix, and references have been made in the text to any major changes effected by the Act. The work of revision has again been undertaken by the second-named of us in consultation with the first-named, the original author. We are grateful to Mr. Alan Cooklin for his help in revising the section on Security of Tenure.

October 1974

E. S. G.
N. H.

EXTRACT FROM PREFACE TO FIRST EDITION

This book is intended to give a practical outline of the land law, or, as it is otherwise known, the law of real property, including the law of wills and intestacy. Its primary purpose is to meet the needs of the many students who are now studying law as part of a wider syllabus. It is hoped that it will also be useful as an introductory book to those who require a more detailed knowledge of the subject: experience has shown that there is much advantage to be gained from studying a short book before proceeding to a more comprehensive work, particularly where the subject is as difficult as is the land law.

March 1st, 1965

E. S. G.

CONTENTS

TABLE OF CASES

ix

TABLE OF STATUTES

CHAPTER 1

THE SCOPE OF THE LAND LAW

THE law of land, or real property, is concerned with the rights, interests and obligations which can exist over land and buildings; how they are created, enforced, assigned and extinguished. Its undoubted complexity is explained by two main factors.

The first lies in the nature of land itself. Land is permanent property, and thus lends itself to the creation of a diversity of concurrent and consecutive interests. The same plot of land or the same house may at once be " owned " [1] by A, let by A to B, sub-let by B to C, and mortgaged by any of them to secure repayment of a loan; it may also be subject to a right of way in favour of one neighbour, whilst in favour of another it may be subject to a restrictive covenant, preventing A and persons claiming through him from building on it. Again, A by his will may direct that the land is to be held in trust for his widow during her life, then for his eldest son during his life, and then for all his grandchildren absolutely in equal shares. To each of these interests it is necessary to apply the appropriate rules, in order to determine its validity and incidents, as to both substance and form. In contrast, other forms of property, such as goods and company shares, are normally the subject of absolute ownership only, and although goods may be let by the owner under a contract of hire or hire-purchase, and personal property generally may be used as security for a loan or may be included, like land, in a family settlement, the normal transaction with such property is an out and out transfer.

The second factor is historical. The foundations of the law of land were laid at a time when land was virtually the sole form of wealth, and formed the basis of the feudal system established after the Norman conquest. The doctrines and rules then developed were appropriate to a feudal society, but they soon acquired a rigidity and formalism which hampered their adaptation to meet the needs of a changing social and economic structure. Although the deficiencies of the common law were in some respects made good by the system of equity administered by the Court of Chancery, and in others by legislation, the result was seldom to simplify, but almost invariably to complicate, the law.

No serious attempt was made to reduce the complexity and obscurity of the land law until the 19th century, when many statutory reforms

---

[1] We shall see that, properly speaking, ownership attaches not to the land itself, but to an estate or interest in the land.

1

were introduced. Finally, sweeping changes were effected by the 1925 property legislation, which came into operation on January 1, 1926. The effect of this legislation, and in particular of the Law of Property Acts 1922 and 1925, the Settled Land Act 1925, the Land Charges Act 1925 [2] and the Land Registration Act 1925, will be considered in due course. As a whole it constitutes a watershed in the land law; it is natural, therefore, to speak of the old law and the new law, or the law before 1926 and the law after 1925.

---

[2] Now repealed and largely re-enacted by the Land Charges Act 1972.

Chapter 2

TENURE AND ESTATE

Tenure

AT common law [1] the ownership of all the land in the country is vested in the Crown. No one other than the Crown can own land. However, other persons may be *tenants, i.e. holders,* of land and have rights in the land which the law will protect even against the Crown. Originally every such person held his land as tenant of some superior feudal lord (who might be the king himself), to whom he owed certain feudal services. There were different *tenures* in the land, *i.e.* different methods of land holding, each of which had its own characteristic services. Thus, if a tenant held by the tenure of knight service he rendered military services to his superior feudal lord, whereas if he held by socage tenure he rendered agricultural services to his lord. By 1925, however, the number of tenures had become so reduced that only two tenures of any importance remained. These were *socage* tenure, otherwise known as freehold, and *copyhold* tenure, formerly known as villeinage. For all practical purposes, by 1925 freehold tenure existed in name only: it had lost its old feudal incidents, and the freehold tenant no longer rendered services to a superior feudal lord. By 1925 freehold tenants almost always held directly of the Crown because it was a rule of the common law that in the absence of evidence of an intermediate lordship (and such evidence was rarely available in 1925) the tenant held directly of the Crown.

Copyhold tenure, on the other hand, remained a living tenure until 1926. The services of this tenure had originally been agricultural, but these services had long since been commuted for annual money payments, known as quit-rents. All copyholds were enfranchised, *i.e.* the tenure was converted into freehold tenure, by the Law of Property Act 1922, as from January 1, 1926. Some of the incidents of this tenure have been permanently preserved, and in particular as a general rule the ownership of any minerals beneath the surface of the land is vested in the former lord or his successor in title—a point that sometimes needs to be watched when buying land even today.

To sum up, there is now only one common law tenure, namely freehold tenure, and this has been shorn of its old feudal incidents, except that former copyhold land is still subject to those few incidents which have been permanently preserved.

---

[1] The common law is the basic, judge-made law of the country.

Estate

The doctrine of estates developed as a corollary of the doctrine of
tenure. Since a *tenant* was not regarded as owning the land itself, it
was necessary to determine what it was that he did own, *i.e.* the
nature and extent of his proprietary interest. His *estate* in the land
accordingly tells us the answer to that question. This in turn depends
upon the terms on which the land was granted to him or to some
predecessor in title of his.

The doctrine of estates has two principal features. First, estates
are classified according to the length of time for which they are
limited to endure; secondly, several persons may simultaneously own
distinct and separate estates in the same piece of land.

Before considering these features, we may notice that the word
estate is also used in two other senses, *viz.* as referring to a particular
plot of land, *e.g.* the Blackacre estate, and as referring to the assets
or property of a deceased person. The sense in which the word is
used in any particular case will appear from the context.

The estates classified

Broadly there are four estates in land, *viz.* (i) the fee simple, (ii)
the fee tail, (iii) the life estate and (iv) the leasehold estate.

(1) *The fee simple*

The word " fee " indicates an estate of inheritance, *i.e.* an interest
in the land that will not necessarily come to an end with the death
of the individual tenant, but is capable of being inherited by another.
The word " simple " indicates that the fee is the ordinary or normal
fee, in contrast to the fee tail. Before 1926 on the death intestate (*i.e.*
without leaving a will) of a tenant in fee simple the land devolved
upon his heir. The heir was ascertained by applying a series of rules
known as the canons of descent. Under these rules the heir might
be found among descendants, ancestors, or collateral relatives (*e.g.*
brothers). If there was no heir the land passed to the superior feudal
lord by a process known as escheat. On a death intestate after 1925
the land will no longer devolve upon the heir, but will be held in
trust for the statutory next of kin, under the Administration of
Estates Act 1925.[2]

As will be seen later, the fee simple owner has for long been
in the position of absolute owner for all practical purposes.

(2) *The fee tail*

A fee tail, or attenuated fee, resembled a fee simple in that on the

---

[2] See Chap. 25.

death of the tenant in tail the land devolved upon his heir, but the fee tail differed from the fee simple in that the heir had to be found amongst descendants of the original tenant in tail; the land could not be inherited by an ancestor or a collateral relative of the original tenant in tail. The position is the same today—this is one of the few cases in which the old canons of descent still apply after 1925.

If upon the death of a tenant in tail it is found that there are no living descendants of the original tenant in tail the fee tail comes to an end. The consequences of this are considered below.

(3) *The life estate*

This explains itself. Land may be granted to a person for his life and his estate then determines with his death. The estate is not one of inheritance. Another form of life estate, known as an estate *pur autre vie*, arises whenever a tenant is entitled to land during the life of another (called the *cestui que vie*). Such an estate determines on the death of the *cestui que vie*, not of the tenant.

(4) *The leasehold estate*

This is the estate enjoyed by a tenant under a lease, *i.e.* a tenant under the modern relationship of landlord and tenant. This relationship is historically distinct from the earlier feudal relationship of lord and tenant. Originally leasehold was not recognised as an estate, but today the law recognises it as both an estate and a tenure. It is an estate because it tells us the duration of the tenant's interest in the land. It is a tenure because it is a method of land holding.

Reversions and remainders

The law allows the owner of an estate in land to confer a lesser estate upon another person, and a reversion then arises. For example, if S, the fee simple owner of Blackacre, grants the land to A for life, S is said to have a reversion because upon the death of A the land will revert to S or, if S is then dead, to his personal representatives, *i.e.* his executors or administrators.

The law also allows a fee simple owner to create a *succession* of estates in the land, and this is called a settlement. For example, S, the fee simple owner of Blackacre, may grant the land to A for his life and thereafter to B for a fee simple estate. B's estate is then said to be a remainder, because upon the death of A the land will remain away from the grantor instead of reverting to him. If upon the death of A, B is already dead the fee simple estate will vest in B's personal representatives. It will be noticed that, whereas a reversion arises by operation of law, a remainder is created by the express terms of the grant.

As a further illustration, S, the fee simple owner of Blackacre, might grant the land to A for life with remainder to B in tail with remainder to C in fee simple. In this illustration, if upon the death of A, B is already dead the fee tail will devolve upon B's heir, found amongst his descendants. If and when the fee tail comes to an end the land will pass to C, or, if he is already dead, his personal representatives.

Both remainders and reversions are future interests, or " reversionary interests " (a much wider and looser expression than reversion in the strict sense). A reversionary interest is any interest in property which will fall into possession in the future.

Reversion has a somewhat different meaning in the context of leaseholds: the lessor's reversion on a lease signifies his estate in the land subject to the lease. This, unlike a reversion under a settlement, is an interest in possession, not a future interest.

CHAPTER 3

CLASSIFICATION OF PROPERTY

THE fee simple, the fee tail and the life estate are freehold estates, *i.e.* estates of fixed but uncertain duration—fixed, in that they are limited to endure for the life of a person, or for the lives of a person and his heirs; uncertain, in that the duration of those lives is uncertain. The leasehold estate is a non-freehold estate, *i.e.* an estate of certain duration, being either for a fixed term or (in the case of a periodical tenancy) determinable by notice.[1] The use of the word "freehold" in this sense is not to be confused with its use in connection with the doctrine of tenures. (In practice the word "freehold" is generally used, even by lawyers, in yet another sense, *viz.* as a synonym for the fee simple estate. Thus, if a man is asked whether he owns the freehold of his house, what is meant is whether he owns a fee simple estate, rather than a mere leasehold.)

Most systems of law divide property into immovables (*i.e.* interests in land) and movables, which include chattels and stocks and shares. The English classification, however, is into *realty* and *personalty*. Realty comprises those forms of property which in the early days of the common law would support a real action, *i.e.* an action by which if he were wrongfully disposed, the owner of the property could recover the property itself (the *res*). Only the freehold estates in land would support such an action and they alone, therefore, are realty. All other forms of property are personalty. Even the leasehold is personalty, because in the early law a leaseholder who was wrongfully dispossessed could not recover the land *in specie*, but only damages, and the terminology has remained unaltered although for centuries the leaseholder has been able to recover the land itself.

---

[1] See Chap. 10.

Chapter 4

WORDS OF LIMITATION

The expression " words of limitation " means the words that are necessary to transfer or create a particular estate in land, such as the fee simple or the fee tail. For example, if A the fee simple owner of Blackacre wishes to transfer the fee simple to B by deed, should the deed say that the land is conveyed to B " in fee simple," or " absolutely," or what expression should be used? [1]

Grants by deed

Before 1926 in order to transfer a fee simple estate in land the grant had to be made to A " and his heirs " or " in fee simple " (words that were first allowed by the Conveyancing Act 1881). No other expressions would suffice, no matter how clear the intention might be, and if the correct expressions were not used only a life estate passed to the grantee. It is important to note that where a grant was made to A *and his heirs,* the words italicised were words of *limitation,* not words of *purchase,*[2] *i.e.* they operated merely to delimit the estate which A was to take, not to grant any estate to his heirs.[3] Of course if A died without having disposed of his estate the heir or heirs would succeed to the land under the old canons of descent; but until then they had no estate, merely a *spes successionis.*

The Law of Property Act 1925, s. 60,. provides that after 1925 a conveyance of land shall pass the whole estate of the grantor to the grantee unless the deed shows a contrary intention. Thus, assuming that the grantor has the fee simple estate in the land a simple conveyance of the land to A without any words of limitation will give the fee simple estate to him, unless the deed shows a different intention.

Before 1926 in order to create a fee tail the grant had to be made to A " and the heirs of his body " (or some similar expression incorporating the word " heirs " and restricting the heirs to descendants of the grantee) or " in tail," words first allowed by the Conveyancing Act 1881. The same strict rule applies today—it has not been relaxed by the Law of Property Act 1925.

---

[1] A conveyance (or transfer) of land must generally be made by deed, *i.e.* a written instrument that has been signed and sealed.

[2] Anyone is a " purchaser " in this sense who acquires the property otherwise than by operation of law.

[3] Under the rule in *Shelley's* case (1581) 1 Co.Rep. 93B, this applied even where the grantor's intention plainly was to grant an estate to the heirs, *e.g.* where a grant was made to A for life with remainder to his heirs. This rule was abolished by the Law of Property Act 1925, s. 131, and the word heirs may now operate as a word of purchase if so intended (see p. 155, *post*).

No words of limitation have ever been necessary in order to transfer a fee simple estate to a corporation aggregate, such as the ordinary limited company, but before 1926 in order to transfer a fee simple estate to a corporation sole, such as a bishop,[4] the words " and his successors " had to be used; otherwise only a life estate passed to whoever was the holder of the office at the date of the grant. The Law of Property Act 1925, s. 60, provides that after 1925 the whole estate of the grantor shall pass to the corporation sole, unless the deed shows a contrary intention.

Gifts by will

The Wills Act 1837, s. 28, provided that the whole estate of a testator in the land should pass to a devisee [5] unless the will showed a contrary intention. This rule remains today. Thus a simple gift of Blackacre " to A " will prima facie give the fee simple to A, if the testator had that estate.

On the death of a testator before 1926 a fee tail could be created by the use of any words in the will which sufficiently showed the intention to do so, *i.e.* the intention to create an estate of inheritance heritable only by descendants of the devisee; " in tail " or " and his descendants " would, for example, suffice. The Law of Property Act 1925, s. 130, provides that on the death of a testator after 1925 the same strict, common law or statutory, expressions shall be used as are required for a deed, *i.e.* " and the heirs of his body " (or some similar expression which includes the word " heirs ") or " in tail."

Failure to use the correct words

Before 1926 if the correct technical expressions required to transfer or create an estate of inheritance were not used in a deed the grantee obtained only a life estate. As has been seen, after 1925 if no words of limitation are used, whether in a deed or a will, the grantee or devisee will prima facie obtain the fee simple estate. But suppose that after 1925, in a deed or a will, words are used which show an *intention* to create a *fee tail*, but fail to do so because they are not the correct technical expressions, what is the result? For example, suppose the fee simple owner of Blackacre leaves it by his will to A " and his descendants," what is the effect? The Law of Property Act 1925 purports to tell us the answer in section 130. It provides in effect that the words are to create the same interest that those words would have created in a grant of personality before 1926. In our

---

[4] Certain institutions, such as the Crown and bishoprics, are regarded as legal persons, distinct from the individual holders of the office.

[5] A *devise* is a gift of *realty* by will; the *devisee* is the donee. A gift of *personalty* by will is called a *legacy* or *bequest*; the donee is called a *legatee*.

example, we are, therefore, to ask ourselves the question what the effect would have been of a gift of personalty before 1926 to A " and his descendants." The answer to the question is uncertain; possibly such a gift would have given the absolute ownership of the personalty to A. If this view is correct the gift by will of realty today to A " and his descendants " gives to A the fee simple estate (as this corresponds to the absolute ownership of personalty). It is certain that the gift will not give a fee tail to A, because before 1926 a fee tail could not subsist in personalty (it can after 1925, as we shall see later).

The life estate and the leasehold

Technical words were not required before 1926 to create a life estate or a lease, nor are they necessary today—words showing the intention are all that is required.

CHAPTER 5

THE CONTRIBUTION OF EQUITY

As with the criminal law and the law of contract and tort, the basis
of the law of real property is common law, but it is in the sphere of
property law that equity [1] has made its most important contribution—
notably, but not exclusively, in its enforcement of the trust (formerly
known as the use). The common law provided no remedy for breach
of trust, so that if S, the fee simple owner of Blackacre, conveyed it
to T in fee simple, directing him to hold it upon trust for B in fee
simple, T at common law was at liberty to disregard the claims of B
and to use the property for his own benefit. The Court of Chancery,
however, at the suit of B (the beneficiary) would enforce the trust
against T (the trustee) and compel T to utilise the property for the
benefit of B. It should be noticed that the Court of Chancery did
not deny T's legal, *i.e.* common law, title to the land, but merely
required T to utilise his ownership of the land for the benefit of B
on the ground that, having undertaken the trust, he was bound in
conscience to do so. It was not long, however, before it was realised
that the effect of compelling T to account to B for all the fruits of
ownership was to make B for many purposes the real owner of the
property.

We are now in a position to understand the meaning of some important terms. The fact that the common law recognises T as the
owner of the land is often expressed by saying that T is the *legal
owner* of the land, or that T has the *legal estate* in the land. The fact
that B has the benefits of ownership is often expressed by saying that
B is the *equitable* (or *beneficial*) *owner,* or that B has the *equitable
estate* in the land.

Originally the Court of Chancery would enforce the trust only
against the trustee himself, and not against any other person into
whose hands the land might come, but in the course of time equity
so enlarged the classes of persons that for one reason or another it
regarded as bound by the trust that in the end the trust became enforceable, not only against the trustee himself, but against any other
person who might acquire the land except a bona fide purchaser for
value of the legal estate without notice, actual or constructive, of the
trust (or any person claiming through such a bona fide purchaser).

---

[1] Like the common law, " equity " is judge-made law; it has its origin in
the activities of the old Court of Chancery. Equity supplemented and cor-
rected the older body of judge-made law known as the common law, which
was administered by other courts. Today the same courts administer both.

11

At first, trusts were of a simple character, *e.g.* a man going on
the crusades might convey his land to trustees for the benefit of his
family during his absence, but in the course of time it became possible
to create a succession of estates under the trust, just as such a succession of estates could be created at common law without a trust. For
example, as we have seen, S, the fee simple owner of Blackacre, might
convey Blackacre to A for life with remainder to B in fee simple,
and A would then have a *legal* life estate and B a *legal* fee simple in
remainder. Alternatively, it now became possible for S to convey
the land to one or more trustees in fee simple directing them to hold
the land upon trust for A for life with remainder to B in fee simple.
A would then have an *equitable* life estate and B an *equitable* fee
simple in remainder. The trustee or trustees had the legal fee simple;
the beneficiaries had equitable estates. In developing the equitable
(or beneficial) interest under the trust in this way, equity borrowed
the common law system of estates. In other words equity allowed
the settlor to create as equitable estates those estates, and only those
estates, that could be created as legal estates at common law without
the employment of a trust. Moreover, to these equitable estates equity
applied nearly all the common law rules governing the particular
estates. For example, on the death of the owner of an equitable fee
simple, or fee tail, the equitable estate would devolve in the same
way as if it had been a legal estate: it would devolve upon the heir,
ascertained by applying the old common law canons of descent. Only
in a few instances did equity decline to " follow the law " in this way.

Apart from equitable interests arising under a trust, equity also
recognised and enforced by means of its own special remedies [2]
certain other interests to which the common law refused to give effect
because due form had not been observed in their creation. In general
any estate or interest in land such as a fee simple, a lease, a mortgage
or an easement was (and still is) valid at law only if granted by deed [3];
and although a contract to create such an interest could be enforced
at law to the extent of recovering damages for its breach, this would
often be an ineffectual remedy. Equity, on the other hand, applying
its maxim that " equity looks on that as done which ought to be
done," treated such a contract as at once creating an equitable interest
in the land; and an attempt to create or convey an interest in land
which failed at law through lack of a deed was treated in the same
way, provided that the grantee had given valuable consideration. Thus,
under a contract for the sale of a fee simple, or for the grant of a
lease or a mortgage or an easement, the purchaser, the lessee, the
mortgagee or the grantee of the easement was regarded *in equity* as

---

[2] Principally the decree of specific performance.
[3] Law of Property Act 1925, s. 52. The rule is much earlier in origin.

having an immediate interest equivalent to a fee simple, lease, mortgage or easement respectively. His interest, however, being merely equitable, was subject to the same defect as indicated above in relation to interests under a trust, namely that it was not enforceable against a purchaser without notice (as we may call him for short).

Three further species of equitable interest may be briefly mentioned here: first the mortgagor's equity of redemption [4]; secondly, the restrictive covenant, the burden of which may in equity (though not at common law) run with the covenantor's land [5]; thirdly a form of interest based upon a principle sometimes referred to as equitable or proprietary estoppel.[6]

We may now compare an equitable interest in land with a legal interest. Every legal right is a right *in rem*, *i.e.* once it attaches to land it binds that land in the hands of everyone who afterwards acquires it, regardless of notice. For example, if A has a legal right of way against the land of B and B sells the land to C, A may still enforce his right against the land, and it is irrelevant that C may have been unaware that the right existed when he acquired the land. But if A's right is merely equitable, it is in theory enforceable only *in personam*, *i.e.* against certain classes of persons: in particular, it will be unenforceable against C if he is a purchaser without notice.

The expression " constructive notice " requires a few words of explanation. A purchaser of land has constructive notice of any interest in the land which he would have discovered if he had made the customary investigation of his vendor's title for the full statutory period (which is now 15 years [7]). This investigation of title involves an inspection of the documents of title to the land for the period in question. A purchaser also has constructive notice of any interest in the land which he would have discovered if he had made those other inquiries and inspections (such as an inspection of the land itself) which a prudent purchaser customarily makes. Further, if a purchaser employs a solicitor or other agent to act for him in acquiring the land, the purchaser has constructive notice of any interest that his agent discovers in that transaction, or would have discovered if he had made the proper investigation of title, inquiries and inspections. This form of constructive notice is sometimes called " imputed notice," because the agent's actual or constructive notice is imputed to the purchaser.

It is still the general rule today that an equitable interest in land

---

[4] See Chap. 19, p. 107.
[5] See Chap. 18, p. 103.
[6] See Chap. 16, p. 96.
[7] Law of Property Act 1969, s. 23, replacing the earlier period of thirty years under the Law of Property Act 1925, s. 44 (1).

is enforceable against everyone except a purchaser without notice, but the 1925 legislation has introduced two far-reaching exceptions. First, beneficial interests subsisting under a trust are now for the most part *overreached* on a sale of land, *i.e.* become detached from the land itself and attached to the proceeds of sale in the hands of the trustees, provided that certain conditions are satisfied.[8] Secondly, most other equitable interests such as equitable leases, equitable easements and restrictive covenants are now *registrable* under the Land Charges Act 1972[9]: if the interest is registered, this is deemed to be actual notice of its existence to everyone acquiring the land or any interest in it[10]; conversely, failure to register the interest renders it void against a later " purchaser " of the land, as that word is defined by the Land Charges Act. Whether the interest is overreached, or is void for non-registration, a purchaser of the land takes free from it even if he has actual notice of it.[11]

The doctrine of notice has retained its importance, however, in relation to those equitable interests which can be neither registered nor overreached.[12]

---

[8] See Chap. 12, pp. 54, 59.
[9] Replacing the Land Charges Act 1925. See Chap. 22.
[10] Law of Property Act 1925, s. 198.
[11] *Ibid.* ss. 2, 199.
[12] For recent examples see *E. R. Ives Investments* v. *High* [1967] 2 Q.B. 379 (C.A.); *Caunce* v. *Caunce* [1969] 1 W.L.R. 286; *Shiloh Spinners Ltd.* v. *Harding* [1973] A.C. 691.

CHAPTER 6

REDUCTION IN THE NUMBER OF LEGAL ESTATES

IT will be evident from what has been said in the last chapter that until 1926 any of the estates (the fee simple, the fee tail, the life estate and the leasehold) could be created either as legal estates or as equitable estates under a trust. After 1925, however, by the Law of Property Act 1925, s. 1, only two estates can subsist as legal estates, *viz.* (i) the fee simple absolute in possession, and (ii) the term of years absolute. These two estates can be created as legal estates (without the employment of a trust) or as equitable estates under a trust. Other estates, such as the life estate, can be created only as equitable interests under a trust.[1]

It will be observed that not every fee simple or term of years can subsist as a legal estate, but only a fee simple absolute in possession or a term of years absolute. The Act contains some technical provisions with regard to the meaning of these expressions for the purposes of section 1, but only a few points need detain us here. The Act (in section 205) provides that " possession " includes receipt of rents and profits of the land, or the right to receive the same, if any. Hence, if the ordinary fee simple owner (or freehold owner, as we generally call him) grants a lease of the land to a lessee, the fee simple remains " in possession " and a legal estate, despite the fact that the lessee acquires the physical possession of the land. But a fee simple which is in remainder is not " in possession " and cannot, therefore, be a legal estate. For example, if land is settled on A for life with remainder to B in fee simple, B's fee simple remainder is an equitable, not a legal, estate.

An estate is not " absolute " if it is conditional or determinable (although there are some exceptions to this for the purposes of section 1). Thus if land is conveyed to S in fee simple until he marries, S's fee simple will not be absolute: it can, therefore, be created only under a trust. On the other hand, an estate is not prevented from being absolute by reason of the fact that it is subject to some other estate. For example, if a freeholder grants a lease his fee simple remains " absolute " despite the fact that it is subject to the leasehold estate of his tenant.

The Law of Property Act 1925, s. 1, also reduces to five the number of rights against the land of another which can subsist as legal interests. These are (i) an easement, right or privilege in or over land

---

[1] As to the form of such trusts, see Chap. 12.

15

for an interest equivalent to an estate in fee simple absolute in possession or a term of years absolute; (ii) a rentcharge in possession issuing out of or charged on land being either perpetual or for a term of years absolute; (iii) a charge by way of legal mortgage; (iv) certain charges on land which are not created by an instrument; (v) rights of entry exercisable over or in respect of a legal term of years absolute, or annexed for any purpose to a legal rentcharge.[2] We shall come across most of these rights in due course.

All other interests which could have been created against the land of another before 1926 can still be created today, but they will be merely equitable, and not legal, interests. It is not necessary to employ a trust in order to create such an equitable interest—the interest will automatically be equitable if it is not in the list of five given above.

It is possible even at this stage to understand why the Act has reduced to five the number of possible legal interests against the land of another. As we have seen, every legal interest gives a right *in rem* and will bind a purchaser of the land affected whether he has notice of it or not. It is, therefore, advantageous to a purchaser that the number of such interests should be reduced to the minimum. When it is considered that this reduction in the number of possible legal interests against the land of another is coupled with provision for the registration, under the Land Charges Act, of many equitable interests and that a purchaser will not be bound by such an interest unless it is registered, it will be appreciated that conveyancing is much safer from the point of view of a purchaser after 1925 than it was before 1926.

Terminology

In the 1925 Acts the term " estate " is retained for the two legal estates and other estates in land are called " interests." This terminology has been generally accepted by legal practitioners. Today, therefore, one normally speaks of a life interest or an entailed interest, rather than a life estate or a fee tail.

We shall now consider the individual estates, or interests, in rather more detail than we have done hitherto.

---

[2] As to equitable rights of entry, see *Shiloh Spinners Ltd.* v. *Harding* [1973] A.C. 691. This case contains a valuable review of the effect of the 1925 legislation in relation to legal and equitable rights in property, and the system of overreaching and registration.

CHAPTER 7

THE FEE SIMPLE

FOR all practical purposes a fee simple owner is today the absolute owner of the land. Nevertheless there are restrictions both at common law and by statute upon the right of the fee simple owner to do as he pleases with the land. For example, at common law he is restrained by the law of tort from using his land in such a way as to cause a nuisance to his neighbours. Again, by statute his liberty to develop the land is severely restricted by the Town and Country Planning Acts 1971 to 1972 (consolidating earlier legislation). This merits a short note.

Town and Country Planning Acts 1971 to 1972

If he wishes to " develop " his land an owner must generally get planning permission from the local planning authority. " Development " is widely defined by the Acts and, besides building operations, includes the working of minerals and the making of any material change in the use to which land (including buildings) is put. For example, it would be development, requiring planning permission, to change the use of a building from that of a dwelling house to that of offices, even though no building work was involved. By way of exception, the Acts provide that certain things are not "development," *e.g.* change of use of buildings if the change is from one purpose to another purpose in the same class specified in the Town and Country Planning (Use Classes) Order 1972. Further the need to obtain planning permission may be dispensed with by the provisions of a General Development Order; for example, the General Development Orders 1973 to 1974 permit the carrying out of building work for agricultural purposes on agricultural land.

We shall now consider some particular rights of the fee simple owner.

Whoever owns the soil. . . .

Whoever owns the soil owns the airspace above the surface and everything beneath the surface. *Cujus est solum ejus est usque ad coelum et ad inferos.* However, there are exceptions to this principle both at common law and by statute. Thus, at common law the Crown is the owner of any gold or silver found in a mine and of treasure trove, *i.e.* any gold or silver coin, plate, or bullion found *concealed* in land (including any building thereon), the owner being unknown.

17

By statute, aircraft have the right of passage through the airspace and
various minerals, such as coal, have been vested in the state or state
agencies.

Whatever is planted in the soil. . . .

Whatever is planted in the soil accedes to the soil, *i.e.* in law it
becomes part of the land. *Quicquid plantatur solo solo cedit.* The
most important application of this principle is in the law of fixtures.
If a chattel is brought on land (including a building thereon) it may
or may not become a fixture. If it becomes a fixture, but not otherwise,
it accedes to the land. The law provides two tests in order to determine
whether a chattel has become a fixture:

(a) *The degree of annexation*

Prima facie if the chattel is securely attached to the land it becomes a fixture, but if it merely rests upon the land by its own weight
it remains a chattel. This test, however, is merely the prima facie
test and determines the burden of proof. It is the second test which is
predominant.

(b) *The purpose of annexation*

If a chattel is brought on or attached to land merely to enable it
to be enjoyed as a chattel it does not become a fixture, and this is
so even if the chattel is securely attached to the land or a building
thereon. Thus in one case [1] tapestry was securely attached to the wall
of a house, but it was held to remain a chattel. On the other hand,
if a chattel is brought on or attached to land for the purpose of im-
proving that land,[2] or as part of a scheme of design or layout, it
becomes a fixture, and this is so even if the chattel rests upon the
land merely by its own weight. Thus in one case [3] stone statues and
seats were placed in a garden as part of a scheme of design of the
garden and were held to have become fixtures although they rested
upon the land merely by their own weight.

It follows from the fact that fixtures are in law part of the land
that a sale of land includes the fixtures unless the contract of sale
provides to the contrary. Again, if land is mortgaged any fixtures
on the land are part of the mortgagee's security and cannot be re-
moved by the mortgagor without the mortgagee's consent. There are,
however, certain exceptional cases in which the owner of a chattel

---

[1] *Leigh* v. *Taylor* [1902] A.C. 157.
[2] But not if the purpose is to accommodate *other* land, *e.g.* where a landowner has the right to lay drains under his neighbour's land, the drains do
not become part of the land under which they are laid (*Simmons* v. *Midford*
[1969] 2 Ch. 415).
[3] *D'Eyncourt* v. *Gregory* (1866) L.R. 3 Eq. 382.

has a right to remove it from the land even though it has become a fixture.

(i) At common law a lessee, before the end of his tenancy, has the right to remove trade, ornamental and domestic fixtures which he has added to the premises. Similarly a tenant for life (or his personal representatives within a reasonable time after his death) has a right to remove similar fixtures as between himself and a remainderman or reversioner. Agriculture, it has been held, is not a trade, so that at common law a lessee or tenant for life has no right to remove agricultural fixtures.

(ii) By the Agricultural Holdings Act 1948, a lessee of an agricultural holding has a statutory right to remove agricultural fixtures before the end of his lease or within two months thereafter. This right is subject to certain conditions, and the landlord may elect to purchase the fixtures at a valuation.

Riparian rights

The owner of the bed of non-tidal water has the riparian rights. When a non-tidal stream flows through land belonging to one person that person is prima facie the owner of the bed of the stream to the extent of his frontage. When a non-tidal stream forms the boundary between two plots of land in the ownership of different persons, the presumption is that the owner of each plot is the owner of the bed up to an imaginary middle line.

The riparian rights include the following:

(a) *Water rights*

A riparian owner has the right to take water from the stream for ordinary purposes connected with his tenement even if thereby he exhausts the stream. Domestic purposes and watering cattle are examples of ordinary purposes. He also has the right to take water from the stream for extraordinary purposes connected with his tenement provided that he returns the water to the stream substantially unchanged in quantity and quality. Manufacturing purposes are prima facie extraordinary. A riparian owner has no right to take water from the stream for purposes unconnected with his tenement. If a riparian owner takes water from the stream in breach of these rules, any lower riparian owner who is injured thereby will have an action against him.

These common law rules are to some extent affected by the Water Resources Act 1963, under which, subject to important exceptions, a licence from the local river authority is required before water can be abstracted from a " source of supply " within the Act.

(b) *Fishing rights*

The riparian owners have the exclusive right to fish in non-tidal water, and the public cannot acquire such a right by long usage.

The Crown is the owner of the bed of tidal water and the public have the right to fish in such water unless the Crown has granted the exclusive right to an individual grantee by an ancient grant known as a franchise of free fishery. The Crown does not possess the right to grant such franchises today.

(c) *Navigation rights*

The riparian owners have the exclusive right to navigate non-tidal water except so far as they have dedicated a right of way to the public. Such a dedication may be presumed from usage by the public to the knowledge of the riparian owners.

Except so far as the right is restricted by statute the public have the right to navigate tidal water.

Foreshore, i.e. the seashore below the ordinary highwater mark, belongs to the Crown or its grantee. Above that mark the presumption is that the shore belongs to the adjoining fee simple owner.

Alienation

At an early date the law recognised the right of a fee simple tenant to alienate (*i.e.* transfer) the land *inter vivos* (during his lifetime). Thus, if land was granted to A and his heirs, A could transfer the land to B and his heirs, thereby giving the fee simple to B, with the result that on the death of B the land would devolve upon B's heir, and not upon A's heir. The ordinary mode of alienation today is by deed. On the other hand, the common law did not recognise the right of a fee simple tenant to dispose of the land by will. This rule was evaded by means of trusts and has long since been abolished by statute; today land can be freely disposed of by will. The formalities of a will are now prescribed by the Wills Act 1837.

CHAPTER 8

THE FEE TAIL

THE fee tail was established as an inalienable freehold estate by the
Statute De Donis 1285, which provided that land granted to a donee
and the heirs of his body should, notwithstanding any alienation by
him, descend to his issue on his death, and revert to the donor when
the donee and all his issue were dead. The result was that the fee
tail, as such, could not be transferred, although, of course, a tenant
in tail in possession of land could transfer to another his own personal
right to occupy the land during his lifetime.

Before the end of the 15th century, however, methods had been
devised for converting a fee tail into a fee simple, and thus barring,
or breaking, the entail.[1] Originally this was done by means of col-
lusive actions, but these actions were abolished by the Fines and
Recoveries Act 1833. This Act substituted a disentailing assurance
(*i.e.* deed of grant) as the means of barring an entail. By this assurance the tenant in tail grants the land to another in fee simple. If the
tenant in tail wishes himself to have the resulting fee simple he directs
that other to hold the land upon trust for himself, or possibly the
tenant in tail may transfer the land to himself in fee simple.

The assurance will convert the fee tail into a full fee simple if
either (a) it is executed by a tenant in tail in possession, or (b) it is
executed by a tenant in tail in remainder with the consent by deed
of the " protector of the settlement," *i.e.* the owner of the first subsisting freehold estate created by the settlement.[2] If the assurance is
executed by a tenant in tail in remainder without the consent of the
protector the fee tail is converted into a base fee, *i.e.* an alienable
fee simple which will last only so long as the fee tail would have
lasted if it had not been barred (in other words so long as there
remain descendants of the original tenant in tail). When the fee tail
is converted into a full fee simple any remainders following the fee
tail are extinguished, but when the fee tail is converted into a base
fee such remainders are unaffected. In neither case are estates preceding
the entail affected. A few examples may make the position clearer.

Suppose that land is settled on A for life with remainder to B in
tail with remainder to C in fee simple, and that B executes a disentailing assurance with the consent by deed of the protector, A. (A's
life estate is a freehold estate and, in the absence of special protectors,

---

[1] Another word for a fee tail.
[2] Before 1926 a settlor could appoint a " special protector," but this power
was abolished by the Law of Property Act 1925.

21

he is the protector.) B's fee tail will be converted into a full fee simple. C's fee simple remainder will be extinguished, but A's preceding life estate will be unaffected. Again, assuming the same settlement, if A has died, B without the consent of anyone may execute a disentailing assurance which will convert his fee tail into a full fee simple. Once again C's remainder will be extinguished. But suppose that A is still alive and that B executes a disentailing assurance without the consent of the protector. B's fee tail will be converted into a base fee. This base fee may be transferred from time to time, but whoever has it will have an estate which will come to an end if at any time B's descendants die out. The land will then go over to C or, if C is then dead, C's personal representatives.

The Act of 1833 remains in force, but the Law of Property Act 1925 has made a number of changes, of which the following may be noticed here:

(i) After 1925 an entail can be created in personalty, such as stocks and shares or leaseholds, as well as in realty.

(ii) Fees tail and base fees can subsist only as equitable interests after 1925.

(iii) After 1925 an entail can be barred by will by a simple gift of the property to a devisee or legatee—the donee will then acquire the fee simple or, if the property is personalty, the absolute ownership. But the Act (in section 176) imposes certain conditions. The will must be made or confirmed by codicil after 1925. The testator must be of full age and at the date of his death he must be tenant in tail in possession—hence a barring by will will always create a full fee simple (or absolute ownership), never a base fee. Further, the will must refer specifically to the particular property or to the instrument under which the testator acquired it or to entailed property generally. Hence a gift of " all my property " to X will not bar an entail, and X will not acquire any entailed property to which the testator was entitled.

Enlargement of base fees

A base fee may become enlarged into a full fee simple in any of the following ways:

(i) By the former tenant in tail executing a fresh disentailing assurance with the consent of the protector or after the protectorship has ceased (*i.e.* after the estates preceding the former entail have come to an end).

(ii) By the owner of the base fee acquiring the fee simple in remainder or reversion.

(iii) By the owner of the base fee remaining in possession of the land for 12 years after the protectorship has ceased. For this reason a base fee will ordinarily come to an end or become enlarged into a full fee simple within a relatively short period of time.

(iv) By a gift of the property by will made by the owner of the base fee if he could have enlarged it during his lifetime without the concurrence of any other person. This power is subject to the conditions laid down by the Law of Property Act 1925, s. 176.

Special types of entail

The inheritance of an entail can be specially restricted by making the grant to male or to female descendants of the grantee, *e.g.* " to A and the heirs male of his body " or " to A in tail male." Further, the inheritance can be restricted to descendants of the grantee and a particular husband or wife, *e.g.* by making the grant " to A and the heirs of his body by his wife Jane ": this is known as a special entail. In such a case if the specified husband or wife dies without issue during the lifetime of the grantee of the entail the grantee becomes " a tenant in tail after possibility of issue extinct " and he can no longer bar the entail.

CHAPTER 9

THE LIFE ESTATE

The doctrine of waste

The law takes the view that a tenant for life has so limited an interest in the land that special restrictions should be imposed upon his right to use the land as he pleases. The rules in question are known as the doctrine of waste. Waste is of three kinds, namely voluntary, permissive and equitable. Voluntary waste is any positive act which alters the land to its detriment, such as felling timber trees, or opening and working a new mine. Permissive waste is allowing the land to deteriorate for want of attention, *e.g.* by failure to maintain buildings in repair. Equitable waste is a special kind of voluntary waste and consists of acts of wanton destruction, such as pulling down or defacing the mansion house or felling trees which have been planted for shelter or ornament.

A tenant for life is impeachable for voluntary waste (*i.e.* he is liable in damages to the remainderman or reversioner if he commits it) unless the settlement makes him unimpeachable. He is unimpeachable for permissive waste unless the settlement makes him impeachable, *i.e.* places him under an obligation to repair. (A tenant for life of a leasehold estate is bound to perform any tenant's repairing covenant in the lease, but this liability is not derived from the doctrine of waste and the liability is not to the remainderman, but to the landlord and the settlor.) A tenant for life is impeachable for equitable waste unless the settlement makes him unimpeachable, and for this purpose it is not sufficient that the settlement makes him unimpeachable for ordinary voluntary waste. If the settlement made a tenant for life unimpeachable for voluntary waste the common law courts would not restrain him from committing acts of wanton destruction, but the Court of Chancery, taking the view that the settlor did not intend the power to commit waste to be abused, would restrain the tenant for life from doing so. This is why waste of this kind is called equitable waste—originally it was restrained only by the court of equity.

The expression " impeachable (or unimpeachable) for waste," without specifying the type of waste, by convention refers to voluntary waste.

A tenant in tail after possibility [1] is impeachable for equitable waste. But with this exception tenants in tail are not impeachable for waste of any kind.

---

[1] See p. 23, *ante.*

Timber

Trees may be timber trees or non-timber trees. Timber trees prima facie are oak, ash and elm trees at least 20 years old, but this definition may be varied by local custom, *e.g.* beech trees are timber in Buckinghamshire.

A tenant for life who is unimpeachable for waste may fell timber or non-timber trees and keep all the proceeds for himself, subject to the doctrine of equitable waste. As we have seen, to fell timber trees is voluntary waste, but if a tenant for life is unimpeachable for such waste he is, of course, at liberty to commit it.

A tenant for life who is impeachable for waste may not, prima facie, fell timber trees. However:

(i) He may take the customary estovers or botes, *i.e.* house-bote (wood required for household purposes), plough-bote (wood required for the repair of agricultural implements) and hay-bote or hedge-bote (wood required for the repair of hedges and fences).

(ii) If the estate is a timber estate (*i.e.* it is used to grow timber commercially) or the custom of the locality permits, he may fell timber in the ordinary course of husbandry and keep all the proceeds for himself. This is not regarded as waste.

(iii) By the Settled Land Act 1925, s. 66, he may in any case fell timber trees with the consent of the trustees of the settlement or the court, but if he relies upon this power the tenant for life will take only one quarter of the proceeds and three quarters will go to the trustees of the settlement as capital money.[2]

A tenant for life who is impeachable for waste may fell non-timber trees that are ripe and suitable for cutting and keep all the proceeds for himself. This is not regarded as waste.

Minerals

If the tenant for life is unimpeachable for waste he may work the minerals and keep all the proceeds for himself. He may open and work a new mine for the purpose if he wishes—to do so is waste, but as he is unimpeachable for waste he may do it.

A tenant for life who is impeachable for waste may continue to work a mine that is already lawfully open and may keep all the proceeds for himself—he does not thereby commit waste. A mine is lawfully open for this purpose if it was opened before the settlement was created, or it was opened by a previous tenant for life who was unimpeachable for waste. A tenant for life who is impeachable for waste may not open and work a new mine.

---

[2] See Chap. 12.

Mining leases

By the Settled Land Act 1925, s. 41, a tenant for life may grant mining leases for periods not exceeding 100 years.[2] A lease granted under this statutory power will be binding on the remainderman or reversioner. In general the tenant for life is entitled to three-quarters of the rent which is payable under such a lease and one quarter goes to the trustees of the settlement as capital money, but if the tenant for life is impeachable for waste and the lessee is authorised to open and work a new mine, the tenant for life takes only one quarter of the rent and three quarters go to the trustees.

Apart from this statutory power, a tenant for life at common law may grant a mining lease authorising the lessee to work minerals to the extent that the tenant for life himself has the right to do so, but such a lease will not be binding on a remainderman or reversioner.

CHAPTER 10

THE LEASEHOLD

The Essentials

THE essentials of a lease are:

(i) Exclusive possession

The grantee must be given exclusive possession of the premises. It is for this reason that a mere lodging agreement is not a lease—the control maintained by the householder is such that a lodger does not obtain exclusive possession of the room which he occupies, and he is a mere licensee.[1] On the other hand the fact that a grantee *is* given exclusive possession of the premises is not conclusive that the transaction is a lease, although it is strong evidence to that effect— the grantee will be a licensee, and not a lessee, if the circumstances negative any intention to create the relationship of landlord and tenant [2] or to create an estate in the land.[3]

(ii) Definite term

The commencement date and the duration of the term must be fixed or determinable. The duration of a periodical tenancy, such as weekly or yearly tenancy, is regarded as determinable by reason of the fact that the term can be brought to an end by the giving by one party to the other of the requisite notice to quit.[4]

Legal and Equitable Leases

In general, if a lease is to be a legal lease (*i.e.* the lessee is to obtain a legal estate), the lease must be granted by deed. As an exception, a lease for three years or less taking effect in possession at the best rent reasonably obtainable without taking a fine (premium) will be a valid legal lease however granted—even if it is granted merely by word of mouth.[5] The exception includes periodical tenancies, such as monthly or yearly tenancies, provided that the basic term does not exceed three years. A lease that is not within the exception given above and not granted by deed is void at law, except that if the tenant goes into possession with the landlord's consent a tenancy at will arises, which will become a periodical tenancy if the landlord

---

[1] For licences see Chap. 16, p. 95.
[2] *Errington* v. *Errington and Woods* [1952] 1 K.B. 290, C.A.
[3] *Barnes* v. *Barratt* [1970] 2 Q.B. 657.
[4] See *Re Midland Railway Company's Agreement* [1971] Ch. 725, C.A.
[5] Law of Property Act 1925, ss. 52–54.

27

accepts rent.[6] In equity, however, an informal lease that would be void at law may be treated as an agreement to grant a lease and thus, on the basis that equity looks upon that as done which ought to be done, as a valid equitable lease. An express agreement for a lease is treated in the same way.[7] As between landlord and tenant, an equitable lease has the same effect as a legal lease, *i.e.* all the obligations created by the agreement or by the informal lease can be enforced by the same means and to the same extent as if they were set out in a properly executed lease. In some respects, however, an equitable lease is not as good as a properly executed legal lease: in particular it requires registration under the Land Charges Act 1972, failing which it will be void against a subsequent purchaser from the landlord.[8]

Different Kinds of Leases

(a) *Leases for a fixed term*

In general, such a lease comes to an end automatically at the end of the agreed term and no notice to quit is required. There are a few exceptions; *e.g.* under the Agricultural Holdings Act 1948, a lease of an agricultural holding for two years or more will not come to an end at the end of the agreed term unless written notice to quit has been given by one party to the other not less than one and not more than two years before the end of the term. Failing such notice the tenancy will continue as a yearly tenancy after the end of the agreed term.

(b) *Yearly tenancies*

A yearly tenancy is otherwise known as an annual tenancy or a tenancy from year to year, *i.e.* the tenancy continues from year to year until one side or the other brings it to an end by serving the requisite notice to quit. Such a tenancy may be created expressly or it may arise by implication of law. It arises by implication of law when the parties to a tenancy do not expressly agree what the nature of the tenancy shall be and the tenant tenders, and the landlord accepts, some payment of an annual rent. For example, if the parties have agreed on the payment of a yearly rent of £100 by four equal quarterly instalments, the payment of a quarter's rent will give rise to a yearly tenancy. A particular case in which a yearly tenancy may arise by implication of law occurs when a tenant under a lease for a fixed term holds over after the end of the term (*i.e.* he remains in

---

[6] See pp. 29, 30, *post.*
[7] This principle has been discussed at pp. 12, 13, *ante.* In its application to leases it is known as the doctrine of *Walsh* v. *Lonsdale* ((1882) 21 Ch.D. 9).
[8] For a further disadvantage, see p. 86, *post.*

possession) and then makes some payment of an annual rent which the landlord accepts. In this particular case the terms of the old lease continue to apply to the new yearly tenancy so far as they are not inconsistent with the nature of such a tenancy.

At common law, in the absence of contrary agreement, in order to determine a yearly tenancy one party must give to the other at least half a year's previous notice expiring at the end of one of the years of the tenancy, *i.e.* expiring on an anniversary of its commencement. But the parties can make what bargain they like unless precluded from doing so by statute. Half a year's notice means 182 days' notice unless the tenancy began on a customary quarter day (Lady Day, Midsummer, Michaelmas, or Christmas), in which case it means the two previous quarters. As an exception to the normal rule a full year's notice expiring on an anniversary of the commencement date is required by the Agricultural Holdings Act 1948, s. 23, for the determination of a yearly tenancy of an agricultural holding, and this rule applies notwithstanding any contrary agreement. Moreover, with a few exceptions, section 2 (1) of the Act converts into a yearly tenancy any periodical tenancy of an agricultural holding which is based on a term of less than a year (and any other letting for an interest less than a tenancy from year to year, *e.g.* a letting for one year certain [9]).

(c) *Other periodical tenancies*

Other periodical tenancies may be created expressly or may arise by implication of law, as in the case of yearly tenancies; for example, if the parties have not agreed upon the nature of the tenancy, but have agreed that a quarterly rent of, say, £25 shall be paid, the payment of a quarter's rent will give rise to a quarterly tenancy.

At common law, subject to contrary agreement, such a tenancy can be brought to an end only at the end of one of the periods of the tenancy, and the length of notice required is the same as that of the period upon which the tenancy is based; for example, if a monthly tenancy began on the 15th of a month it can be brought to an end on the 15th of any month, and for this purpose notice to quit must have been given at least one month before that date. Although in general the parties can vary the common law rule by special agreement, the Rent Act 1957, s. 16,[10] provides that where the letting is of a dwelling notice must be given at least four weeks before the date on which the tenancy is to determine, and this provision applies notwithstanding any contrary agreement. It should be understood that

---

[9] *Bernays* v. *Prosser* [1963] 2 Q.B. 592, C.A.
[10] This provision, being of general application, is *not* repealed by the Rent Act 1968.

the Act does not *reduce* the length of notice required where under the common law rule a longer period of notice is necessary.

(d) *Tenancies at will and at sufferance*

A tenancy at will is one which is to continue so long as it is the will of both parties that it shall do so. It is obvious that such a tenancy will come to an end as soon as either party gives notice to quit. It will also come to an end if either party does an act which is inconsistent with the continuance of the tenancy, *e.g.* if the tenant commits voluntary waste.

A tenancy at sufferance, which is not perhaps a true tenancy, arises when a tenant without the landlord's consent holds over after a previous tenancy has come to an end. A tenant at sufferance is bound to pay compensation to the landlord for his occupation of the land. Moreover tenants who hold over after notice to quit has been given are liable to certain statutory penalties, payable to the landlord.

(e) *Leases for lives, etc.*

A lease for a life or lives or for a term of years determinable with a life or lives or on the marriage of the lessee (*e.g.* a lease for 50 years which, the lease provides, shall come to an end automatically on the death of a specified person or on the lessee's marriage) is converted by the Law of Property Act 1925, s. 149,[11] into a lease for 90 years. After the end of the life or lives or the marriage of the lessee either party may determine this lease by giving at least one month's notice expiring on any quarter day which is applicable to the tenancy, or if there are no such quarter days any customary quarter day. This provision applies only to leases at a rent or in consideration of a fine.

(f) *Perpetually renewable leases*

Another curious provision, this time in the Law of Property Act 1922, applies to perpetually renewable leases, *i.e.* leases which give to the tenant a perpetual right of renewal. For example, a lease for seven years may provide that the tenant shall have the right, not less than one month before the end of the term, to require the landlord to grant a new lease for seven years upon the same terms, including the provision for renewal, as the original lease. The Act converts such leases into terms of 2,000 years, determinable by the *lessee* by the giving of at least 10 days' notice expiring on any date on which, but for the Act, the lease would have come to an end if it had not been renewed, *i.e.* in the example given above the end of any seven-year term. If the lease provides for payment of a fine on renewal, then (a) if the lease was granted before 1926, the fine is commuted into additional rent,

---

[11] Applying to leases granted whether before 1926 or after 1925.

but (b) if the lease was granted after 1925, the provision for payment of the fine is void.

We may also notice here another provision of the 1922 Act which renders void any contract made after 1925 to renew an existing lease for more than 60 years after its termination.

(g) *Future leases*

The Law of Property Act 1925, s. 149, renders void the grant after 1925 of a lease which is to take effect more than 21 years after the date of the grant. The same section invalidates a contract to grant such a lease, *i.e.* a lease which is to commence more than 21 years from the grant of the lease; the provision does not invalidate a contract to grant a lease which is to start more than 21 years from the date of the *contract*.[12]

We have already seen that a lease may come to an end by effluxion of time or may be determined by the service of notice to quit in certain cases. We must now consider some other ways in which a lease may come to an end.

Forfeiture

In the curious language of lawyers a landlord is said to forfeit a lease when he exacts a forfeiture of it by reason of the tenant's breach of some obligation which rests upon him. In general, if a landlord wishes to have this right of forfeiture for breach by the tenant of his obligations, or any of them, he must stipulate for the right in the lease; the law does not confer such a right upon the landlord even if the tenant falls into arrears with his rent. The landlord may stipulate for the right either by providing in the lease that the tenant's perform-ance of his obligations is a condition of the lease or by inserting into the lease an express condition of re-entry, *i.e.* a provision that the landlord may re-enter and determine the lease upon the breach by the tenant of his obligations.

Waiver

If a landlord has the right of forfeiture he may lose it in respect of a particular breach of the lessee's obligations by waiving the right. Waiver may be express or it may be implied. There is usually an implied waiver if the landlord with knowledge of a breach does any act showing that he has elected to treat the lease as still in existence, *e.g.* by claiming rent accruing due after the breach,[13] or by distraining for rent accruing due whether before or after the breach (the act of

---

[12] *Re Strand and Savoy Properties Ltd.* [1960] Ch. 582.
[13] See *Central Estates (Belgravia) Ltd.* v. *Woolgar (No. 2)* [1972] 1 W.L.R. 1048, C.A.

distraining shows an election to treat the lease as still in existence, because the remedy of distress [14] can be used by a landlord only so long as the relationship of landlord and tenant subsists). But a landlord's claim for possession on the ground of breaches of covenant is not inconsistent with an alternative claim for an injunction restraining further breaches, and the two may properly be joined in the same action.[15]

Restrictions on right of forfeiture

Even if a landlord has a right of forfeiture for breach of a tenant's obligation the law imposes certain restrictions upon its exercise.

(a) Forfeiture for non-payment of rent

At common law a landlord cannot exercise a right of re-entry for non-payment of rent unless he has made a formal demand for the rent upon the premises before sunset on the last day on which the rent has to be paid in order to avoid forfeiture; and this demand must continue until sunset. However, the terms of the lease may exempt the landlord from the need to make this formal demand, and the Common Law Procedure Act 1852 exempts him from doing so if half a year's rent is in arrears and unpaid and there are no sufficient chattels upon the premises to enable the landlord to recover the rent by distress.

A tenant may ask the court to grant him relief against a forfeiture which he has incurred for non-payment of rent, *i.e.* may ask that his lease be restored to him. The court has a discretionary power to grant such relief; the power is equitable in origin but is now regulated by the Common Law Procedure Act 1852. Under this Act the tenant must make his application for relief within six months of ejectment.[16]

(b) Forfeiture for breach of other obligations

The Law of Property Act 1925, s. 146, contains certain general provisions which apply to forfeiture for breach of a tenant's obligations other than to pay rent and other than certain obligations which are specially mentioned below. Under this section the landlord is required to serve a statutory notice upon the tenant and to give him a reasonable time within which to comply with it; if the tenant does comply he avoids forfeiture. Moreover, under the same section, the court may grant relief against forfeiture if the tenant makes his application before the landlord obtains possession of the premises. The

---

[14] This consists in seizing and selling the tenant's chattels for the purpose of recovering arrears of rent.

[15] *Calabar Properties Ltd.* v. *Seagull Autos Ltd.* [1969] 1 Ch. 451.

[16] It seems this limit does not apply where forfeiture is enforced by peaceable re-entry, not by court proceedings (*Thatcher* v. *C. H. Pearce & Sons (Contractors) Ltd.* [1968] 1 W.L.R. 748).

landlord generally sues for possession and the tenant usually makes his application for relief in the landlord's action.

The statutory notice must (i) specify the breach complained of, (ii) require the tenant to remedy it, if it is capable of remedy, and (iii) require the tenant to make compensation in money (if the landlord requires that). If the breach is incapable of remedy (as may be the breach of a tenant's covenant not to assign or sublet without consent) the landlord need allow the tenant only a short time, e.g. a fortnight, before he proceeds to enforce the forfeiture.[17]

There are special provisions where the notice relates to breach of a repairing covenant. In particular, by the Leasehold Property (Repairs) Act 1938,[18] if a lease is for seven years or more, of which at least three remain unexpired, the notice must inform the tenant of his right to serve a counter notice under the Act, and if the tenant does this within 28 days the landlord cannot proceed further without the leave of the county court.

It may also be noticed here that under section 147 of the Law of Property Act 1925 the court in its discretion may relieve a tenant from liability under a covenant for internal decorative repair.

(c) *Forfeiture for breach of inspection covenants in mining leases*

The rent payable under a mining lease is usually in the form of a royalty which varies with the amount of the mineral got by the tenant under the lease. The lease generally contains detailed provisions requiring the tenant to keep proper accounts and giving to the landlord a right of inspection of the accounts and of the working of the mine. Parliament has recognised the vital importance of such provisions to the landlord by enacting that the Law of Property Act 1925, s. 146, shall have no application to a breach by the tenant of such inspection covenants. In the event of a breach by the tenant of such provisions, therefore, the landlord may forfeit the lease without serving the usual statutory notice and the court has no power to grant relief to the tenant.

(d) *Forfeiture on the bankruptcy, etc. of the tenant*

The lease may contain provisions which allow the landlord to re-enter if the tenant becomes bankrupt or suffers the lease to be taken in execution. (A lease may be a valuable asset and a creditor of the tenant who obtains judgment against him may by means of the appropriate writ of execution sell the tenant's interest in the lease for

---

[17] *Scala House and District Property Co. Ltd.* v. *Forbes* [1973] 3 W.L.R. 14, C.A., *cf. Rugby School (Governors)* v. *Tannahill* [1935] 1 K.B. 87, C.A.
[18] As amended by the Landlord and Tenant Act 1954, s. 51 (1). These provisions also apply where a landlord claims damages for breach of a repairing covenant.

what it will fetch. This is what is meant by the tenant's suffering the lease to be taken in execution.) Section 146 provides that in the case of certain types of property the section shall have no application to the exercise by a landlord of his right of re-entry on these grounds. These cases are where the lease is of (i) agricultural or pastoral land, (ii) mines or minerals, (iii) a public-house, (iv) a furnished house, or (v) property with respect to which the personal qualifications of the tenant are of special importance to the landlord. In any other case the section applies for one year after the bankruptcy or taking in execution, and it applies indefinitely after the end of the year if during the year the lease has been sold by the tenant's trustee in bankruptcy or execution creditor; but if at the end of the year the lease has not been so sold the section ceases to apply, with the result that the landlord may re-enter without serving the usual statutory notice and the court has no power to grant relief against the forfeiture.

Sub-tenants

If a head lease is forfeited any sub-lease automatically falls to the ground. However, the Law of Property Act 1925, s. 146, as amended by the Law of Property (Amendment) Act 1929, gives to a sub-tenant the right to apply to the court for relief against the forfeiture of the head lease, whatever the ground may be on which the head lease has been forfeited (*i.e.* even if the head lessee himself could not have applied for relief against the forfeiture). The court may then order the grant to the sub-tenant of a lease for a term not exceeding the unexpired residue of the sub-lease. This new lease will generally be between the head landlord and the sub-tenant, who will thus become a head tenant under the new lease. When a head lease has been forfeited for non-payment of rent a sub-tenant has a separate right to apply for relief against the forfeiture under the terms of the Common Law Procedure Act 1852.

Other Modes of Determination

A lease will also come to an end if the tenant surrenders it to his landlord and the landlord accepts the surrender. Surrender may be express, in which case it should be by deed, or it may be implied by law, *e.g.* if the tenant gives up possession of the premises to the landlord and the landlord accepts that possession. If a lessee who has granted a sub-lease surrenders his lease to his landlord (L), the sub-lease will not be extinguished and L will take subject to it.

A lease may also come to an end by merger. Merger occurs when the owner of the lease acquires the reversion, in which case the lease is said to merge in the reversion, and it ceases to exist.

Finally, it may be mentioned that the Law of Property Act 1925,

s. 153, allows a lessee to execute a deed of enlargement enlarging his lease into the fee simple. The principal conditions are that the lease should have been granted for at least 300 years, of which 200 years or more remain unexpired, that no rent of any money value should be payable, and that no trust or right of redemption should exist in favour of the reversioner. A mortgage, for example, is generally made, as we shall see,[19] by granting to the mortgagee a term of 3,000 years. If the mortgagor loses his right of redemption (*i.e.* his right to recover his property on payment off of the loan) the mortgagee may execute a deed of enlargement enlarging his term of years into the fee simple.[20]

Security of Tenure

Special legislation will often prevent a landlord from requiring a tenant to leave the premises even though the lease has come to an end under the rules which we have outlined above. For convenience these provisions are considered at the end of this chapter.

Implied Obligations of Landlord and Tenant

Certain obligations are imposed upon the landlord or the tenant by implication of law. In general, these implied obligations may be varied by express provisions in the lease, but in some instances variation is prohibited by statute.

1. Landlord's obligations

(a) *Implied covenant for quiet enjoyment*

The landlord impliedly covenants that the tenant shall have quiet enjoyment of the premises free from any interference by the landlord or anyone lawfully claiming through the landlord. It will be observed that the covenant is in a restricted form. If, for example, the lease in question is a sub-lease and the sub-lessor loses his own lease by the exercise by the superior landlord of a right of re-entry, the sub-lessee will not be able to sue the sub-lessor (his own landlord) for damages for breach of the sub-lessor's implied covenant for quiet enjoyment. The sub-lessee has not been disturbed in his possession of the premises by any act of his landlord or anyone claiming lawfully through his landlord—the superior landlord does not claim through his own tenant (the sub-lessor), but by title paramount. (As we have seen [21] the sub-lessee's remedy in this case is to apply to the court for relief against the forfeiture of the head lease.)

It is uncertain precisely what acts will amount to a breach of a covenant for quiet enjoyment. It has been generally considered that

---

[19] See Chap. 19.
[20] Law of Property Act 1925, s. 88 (3), and see pp. 108, 125, *post.*
[21] p. 34, *ante.*

the acts must amount to a physical interference with the tenant's possession of the land, but this has been doubted.[22]

(b) *Derogation from grant*

Like any other grantor, a landlord is not at liberty to derogate (*i.e.* detract) from his grant. He must not therefore do, or suffer to be done, anything which would render the premises unfit for the purposes for which they have been let.

(c) *Condition of the premises*

In general it is not a condition of a lease that the premises are fit for occupation, nor does the landlord undertake to maintain them in repair. There are, however, some exceptions:

(i) *Furnished houses.* On the letting of a house furnished there is (unless otherwise agreed) an implied condition that the premises are reasonably fit for human habitation at the commencement of the lease (but the landlord does not undertake to keep them so). This common law rule is known as the rule in *Smith* v. *Marrable*.[23]

(ii) *Housing Act 1957.* Under section 6 of this Act when a house is let at a rent which does not exceed £80 a year in London or £52 a year elsewhere (half these amounts if the tenancy was granted before July 6, 1957) there is an implied condition that the premises are fit for human habitation at the commencement of the tenancy, and the landlord impliedly agrees to keep them so. The parties cannot generally contract out of these provisions. It may be mentioned that quite a small defect may amount to a breach of the landlord's obligation where, as in the case of a broken sash-cord, it is such as to render the premises dangerous. But a landlord incurs no liability in respect of a defect unless he had notice of it, and this rule applies even where the defect was latent so that the tenant could not have notified the landlord of it (the same rule applies when a landlord expressly covenants to keep the premises in repair).

(iii) *Housing Act 1961.* By sections 32 and 33 of this Act if a lease of a dwelling house is granted after October 24, 1961, for less than seven years (or the landlord can determine the lease within seven years) there is an implied covenant by the landlord to keep the structure and exterior of the premises, including the drains, in repair, and to maintain the installations for the supply of gas, water, and electricity, for sanitation and for space and water heating. When this provision applies any liability in respect of these matters which would otherwise

---

[22] *Kenny* v. *Preen* [1963] 1 Q.B. 499, C.A. It is now a criminal offence unlawfully to evict or harass the occupier of residential premises (Rent Act 1965, s. 30).

[23] (1843) 11 M. & W. 5 (premises bug-ridden).

have rested on the tenant is excluded. The parties cannot contract out of these provisions without the leave of the county court.

It may be mentioned here that local authorities have wide statutory powers under which they may compel the owner of a house to maintain it in reasonable condition, so that a tenant by complaining to the local authority may sometimes be able to compel his landlord to do work which as between himself and the tenant he is not contractually bound to do.

2. Tenant's obligations

A tenant is bound to pay the rent, to pay tenants' rates and taxes (*i.e.* all ordinary rates and taxes), and if the landlord is liable to repair the premises to allow the landlord to enter and view the state of repair.

Tenants generally are impeachable for voluntary waste. A tenant for a fixed term is also impeachable for permissive waste, so that he is under a general obligation to maintain the premises in repair. Periodical tenants are not impeachable for permissive waste, but are bound to use the premises in a tenant-like manner (*e.g.* to keep the drain pipes clear), and a yearly tenant may perhaps be bound to keep the premises wind and water tight.[24]

The " Usual Covenants "

The grant of a lease is sometimes preceded by the signing of an agreement to grant the lease. Such an agreement may expressly provide that the lease shall contain the usual covenants, and if the agreement is silent as to what covenants the lease shall contain it is an implied term of the agreement that the lease shall contain the usual covenants. What covenants are usual is then a matter of evidence and depends upon the practice of conveyancers in the locality, but the following covenants are usual by the general custom of conveyancers[25]:

(a) On the part of the landlord, a covenant for quiet enjoyment, restricted to the acts of the landlord and those lawfully claiming through him.

(b) On the part of the tenant, covenants to pay the rent and to pay tenants' rates and taxes, to keep the premises in repair, and to permit the landlord to enter and view the state of repair.

(c) A condition of re-entry for non-payment of rent.

If the parties have expressly or impliedly agreed that the lease shall contain the usual covenants, then when the lease comes to be

---

[24] See generally *Warren* v. *Keen* [1954] 1 Q.B. 15, C.A.
[25] *Hampshire* v. *Wickens* (1878) 7 Ch.D. 555; *Hodgkinson* v. *Crowe* (1875) 10 Ch.App. 622.

drawn up either party may insist upon the inclusion of the usual covenants and may prevent the insertion of any other covenant.

Express Covenants

Mention may be made here of two express covenants that are commonly found in leases:

Covenant to repair

The main principle which applies to the interpretation of such a covenant is that it is a covenant to repair, and not to re-build, the premises. The covenantor is bound by timely repair to maintain the premises in as good a condition as possible, regard being had to the age and condition of the premises at the commencement of the tenancy; but he is not bound to rebuild main parts of the structure which have become beyond ordinary repair. The covenant does, however, extend to the replacement of *subsidiary* parts of the premises which have got beyond ordinary repair.

The addition to the word " repair " of such expressions as " tenant-able " or " good and substantial " seems to have little if any, effect.

Sometimes a covenant to repair is qualified by the addition of some such words as " fair wear and tear excepted." Such excepting words are restrictively construed by the courts, and although they will exempt the tenant from the immediate consequences of the excepted cause they will not exempt him from consequential damage. For example, if a slate blows off the roof, the tenant is not immediately liable to replace it, but if he does not prevent the entry of rain and the rain causes the roof timbers to rot, the tenant will be liable for the damage to the timbers.[26]

By the Landlord and Tenant Act 1927, s. 18, the damages recoverable by a landlord may not exceed the injury to the reversion. Hence if at the end of the tenancy the landlord intends to pull down the premises he can recover nothing.[27]

Covenant against assigning, etc.

The lessee often covenants not to assign or under-let the premises. If the covenant is in this simple form, only an *inter vivos* disposition of the whole of the premises will amount to a breach; an under-letting of part of the premises will not, therefore, be a breach. It is rare, however, to find a covenant in this simple form, and it often requires the tenant not to assign or under-let or part with possession

---

[26] *Regis Property Co. Ltd.* v. *Dudley* [1959] A.C. 370.
[27] For a further restriction on the landlord's rights, see the Leasehold Property (Repairs) Act 1938 (*ante*, p. 33).

of the premises or any part thereof. It is an unsettled question whether a covenant not to under-let is broken by the letting of lodgings.

If the covenant is not to assign or sub-let *without the landlord's consent*, two statutory provisions come into operation. First, by the Law of Property Act 1925, s. 144, subject to contrary agreement, the landlord may not demand a fine as the price of his consent. Secondly, by the Landlord and Tenant Act 1927, s. 19, notwithstanding any contrary agreement, the landlord may not unreasonably withhold his consent. (Section 19 also provides that in the case of building leases for more than 40 years, of which more than seven remain unexpired, the landlord's consent is not required for an assignment or sub-letting.) There is no hard and fast rule as to the matters which a landlord may properly consider in deciding whether or not to grant his consent, but the personality of the proposed tenant and the nature of the proposed user of the premises are clearly relevant considerations. If consent is requested, and is unreasonably refused, the tenant will incur no liability by assigning without consent. But he will be in breach if he assigns without having sought consent, even though the assignment is one to which consent could not reasonably have been refused.

Security of Tenure and Rent Restriction

The Rent Act 1968

This Act consolidates (*i.e.* repeals and largely re-enacts) a long series of statutes commonly known as the Rent Acts of which the first was passed in 1915 and the last in 1965. The Act has two main objects—first to give security of tenure to the tenant and secondly to restrict the amount of the rent that the landlord may lawfully charge. The main provisions of the Act apply to any tenancy under which a dwelling-house (which may be part of a house) is let as a separate dwelling, provided in most cases that the dwelling-house has a rateable value not exceeding £1,500 in London or £750 elsewhere.[28] So long as the initial lease or agreement remains in force such a tenancy is called a " protected tenancy."

As judicially interpreted, the Act does not apply where the premises have been let solely for business purposes [29]; furthermore (for reasons concerned with user rather than purpose) the majority of mixed business–residential lettings, *e.g.* a small shop with rooms above, also fall outside the Act.[30] The requirement that the dwelling should be *separate* prima facie excludes shared accommodation; but a distinction is drawn between the tenant obliged to share with his landlord and

---

[28] s. 1 as amended by the Counter-Inflation Act 1973, s. 14.
[29] Nor where the purpose is to provide more than one dwelling (*Horford Investments Ltd.* v. *Lambert* [1973] 3 W.L.R. 872, C.A.).
[30] " Controlled tenancies " are an exception.

the tenant obliged to share with others. The former has the more limited protection afforded in relation to furnished lettings by Part VI of the Act [31]; the latter enjoys the main benefits of the Act with only minor modifications.

The Act is also excluded (a) where no rent is payable or where the rent is less than two-thirds of the 1965 rateable value of the property, (b) where the rent bona fide includes payments in respect of board, attendance or the use of furniture, provided as regards attendance and the use of furniture that the amount of rent fairly attributable thereto forms a substantial portion of the whole rent (but again in case (b), the tenant may have protection under Part VI),[32] or (c) in general where the tenancy relates to an agricultural holding. Finally the Act does not apply where the landlord is the Crown or a Government department or a local authority, development corporation, housing trust or similar body (although in such cases a sub-tenancy may be protected).

Tenancies subject to the Act include both a " controlled tenancy " and a " regulated tenancy." A controlled tenancy is one which was subject to the old Rent Acts under the law as it stood between the Rent Act 1957 (which de-controlled many tenancies) and the Rent Act 1965 (which restored and greatly extended the protection of tenancies). A regulated tenancy (an expression first introduced by the 1965 Act) is any protected tenancy other than a controlled tenancy.[33]

The provisions of the 1968 Act with regard to security of tenure are broadly the same for both controlled and regulated tenancies. The Act gives to the tenant the right to continue in possession of the premises after his contractual tenancy has come to an end, *e.g.* by service of notice to quit. This new tenancy is generally known as a statutory tenancy, and those terms of the contractual tenancy which are not inconsistent with the Act apply to the new tenancy. This statutory tenancy, however, is a legal anomaly because the right to remain in possession is personal to the tenant, and he cannot dispose of it *inter vivos* or by his will (although there is provision whereby the tenant has a limited power with the landlord's consent to substitute another tenant in his place). On the tenant's death, his right is transmitted to his widow residing with him at his death, or if there is no widow so residing then tó some other member of his family who had resided with him for six months before his death.

---

[31] See p. 42, *post.*
[32] Important modifications are made by the Rent Act 1974: see Appendix.
[33] Provision is made for the conversion of controlled into regulated tenancies (Housing Finance Act 1972, s. 35), and it is expected that this process will have been completed by the end of 1975.

Before the Rent Act 1965 there could be only one such transmission, but a second transmission is now possible. A statutory tenancy subsists only so long as the tenant (or his successor) resides on the premises.

Once the tenant has become a statutory tenant, there are certain grounds upon which the landlord may obtain an order for possession upon application to the county court, *e.g.* on the ground that the tenant has broken certain of his obligations; or that the tenancy was a service tenancy (*i.e.* the premises were let to the tenant in consequence of his former employment by the landlord) and the premises are reasonably required as a residence for another servant of the landlord; or that the landlord reasonably requires the premises as a residence for himself, his son or daughter over 18, or his father or mother, provided that he did not become a landlord " over the tenant's head " by purchase after March 23, 1965, and that the tenant is unable to satisfy the court that in all the circumstances greater hardship would be caused by making the order for possession than by refusing it. In all cases the court must be satisfied that in all the circumstances it is reasonable to make an order for possession. If the tenancy is a regulated tenancy, there are certain exceptional cases where a landlord is entitled to recover possession as of right without proof of reasonableness.

The amount of rent that the landlord may lawfully charge under a protected tenancy is restricted, but it is in this respect that the Act differentiates significantly between controlled tenancies and regulated tenancies. For controlled tenancies there is a *rent limit* which is based on the aggregate of the gross value of the premises for rating purposes on November 7, 1956, plus other items, such as the annual rates if borne by the landlord, and any service charge or charge for furniture, multiplied by a factor which varies with the respective liability of the parties for repairs. This rent limit may be raised in certain circumstances, *e.g.* where a change occurs during any rental period with regard to the provision of services or furniture by the landlord, or where the landlord effects an improvement in the premises. For regulated tenancies the rent recoverable is that registered for the dwelling-house in accordance with the provisions of the Act, or, if no such rent is registered, the rent payable under the present tenancy. Applications for registration of a rent may be made to the rent officer by the landlord or by the tenant or jointly by both. There is nothing to prevent a tenant from agreeing to a rent on one day and applying to the rent officer on the next. The rent officer registers the rent if he thinks it fair, or, if not, determines and registers a *fair rent*. If either party objects, the matter is referred to a rent assessment committee. In determining a fair rent, regard must be had " to all the circumstances (other than personal circumstances) and in particular to the age, character and locality of the dwelling-house and to its state of repair ": the fact of scarcity of accommodation is expressly excluded from consideration.

Furnished lettings [34]

As we have seen, a tenancy under which the rent includes a substantial payment for the use of furniture or services or under which the tenant shares living accommodation with the landlord is not a protected tenancy within the main provisions of the Rent Act. But in these cases a limited protection is given by Part VI of the Act (replacing similar provisions in the Furnished Houses (Rent Control) Act 1946, as amended). Part VI applies only to dwellings of which the rateable value is within the limits set by the Act, and it is excluded if any substantial payment is made for board. Subject to these limitations, protection is given not only to a tenant under a lease, but also to a lodger or paying guest provided he has exclusive occupation [35] of some part of the premises. The protection given is twofold. First the contract of tenancy may be referred (by either party or by the local authority) to the local rent tribunal, which may confirm the rent or reduce it, but cannot increase it except in respect of any increased cost of services. Rents so determined are registered, and the landlord may not thereafter charge any greater rent than the registered rent unless the rent tribunal authorises an increase on the ground of a subsequent change of circumstances. Secondly, a tenant who has referred his contract of tenancy to a tribunal is given security of tenure for a period of six months after the decision of the tribunal or for such shorter period as the tribunal may direct, and by taking appropriate action the tenant may obtain successive extensions of his security of tenure for periods of not more than six months at a time.

Security of tenure can only be obtained where the tenancy does not expire by effluxion of time and where the contract of tenancy has been referred to a tribunal (whether before or after service of a notice to quit, but before expiry of the period at the end of which the notice takes effect). Furthermore, there is in general no security where the landlord is an owner-occupier (*i.e.* has previously occupied the dwelling as his residence) and requires the dwelling again as a residence for himself or his family.

---

[34] Important changes have been made by the Rent Act 1974: see Appendix.
[35] Not "exclusive possession" in the technical sense (see p. 27, *ante*): *Luganda* v. *Service Hotels Ltd.* [1969] 2 Ch. 209.

Long tenancies of dwelling-houses

The old Rent Acts did not apply to tenancies for a term exceeding 21 years, but a limited security was given by Part I of the Landlord and Tenant Act 1954. Such tenancies, however, if not at a low rent (*i.e.* a rent less than two-thirds of the rateable value of the property) are now governed by the Rent Act 1968. In determining whether a long tenancy is at a low rent, such part of the rent (if any) as is expressed to be payable in respect of rates, services, repairs, maintenance or insurance is to be disregarded, unless it could not have been regarded by the parties as so payable.[36]

If the tenancy is at a low rent, it is outside the Rent Act, but remains subject to the Landlord and Tenant Act 1954 provided that the *only* reason why the Rent Act does not apply is the low rent. Under the 1954 Act, the tenancy is automatically continued after the end of the term if the tenant so desires, and the landlord may terminate it in only two ways. First, after service of notice he may apply to the court for possession on grounds similar to those under the Rent Act. Secondly, he may serve a notice proposing a statutory tenancy, in which case the terms of the tenancy will be settled by agreement between the parties or by the court. After commencement of the statutory tenancy, the rent will be governed by the provisions of the Rent Act 1968.

If the lease is of a house to which the Leasehold Reform Act 1967 applies, the tenant may wish alternatively to take advantage of the provisions of that Act (see below).

Leasehold enfranchisement

Leases for a very long term such as 99 years or 999 years are frequently granted at a low, or " ground," rent in consideration either of the tenant building on the land or (where there is already a building on the land) of his paying a " fine " or premium virtually equivalent to the capital or freehold value of the land. The tenant (including of course his successors in title) at the end of such a lease had no security of tenure, because the tenancy, being at a low rent, was excluded from the operation of the Rent Acts. The Leasehold Reform Act 1967 meets this case by giving to the tenant of a leasehold house of a 1965 rateable value of not more than £200 (or £400 in London) held for a term exceeding 21 years at a rent less than two-thirds of the rateable value a right to acquire on fair terms the freehold or an extended lease (of 50 years), provided that when he seeks to exercise the right he has occupied the house as his residence for the

---

[36] Housing Act 1969, s. 80. By s. 81, certain long tenancies which' *are* within the Rent Act may nevertheless be sold, and are exempt from the premium restrictions imposed by the Rent Act.

last five years or for periods amounting to five years in the last 10 years. If the tenant elects to purchase the freehold, the price is based on the market value of the land disregarding the value of the buildings on it. If he claims a new lease, the rent is to be the current letting value of the site without the buildings, and may be revised after 25 years. In certain cases the landlord may oppose the tenant's claim (*e.g.* if the landlord proposes to demolish or reconstruct the house, or if he reasonably requires the house as a residence for himself or a member of his family), but only at the cost of compensating the tenant for the loss of his rights under the Act. The 1967 Act applies only to a " house," and for this purpose a flat is not a house.[37] The tenant of a flat under a long tenancy at a low rent thus has no rights under the 1967 Act and no protection under the Rent Act, but he will have the limited protection still afforded by Part I of the Landlord and Tenant Act 1954.[38]

Business premises

Most tenancies of business premises (including mixed business-residential premises)[39] are protected by Part II of the Landlord and Tenant Act 1954. The broad effect of the Act is to continue the existing tenancy indefinitely unless and until terminated in accordance with the provisions of the Act. These require service by the landlord of a statutory notice to quit, which in turn gives the tenant the right to claim a new lease.

In default of agreement between the parties the tenant will have to apply to the court for his new tenancy, but unless the landlord can establish one of certain statutory grounds set out in his notice, the court will be bound to grant a new tenancy for a period not exceeding 14 years on such terms as it thinks fit having regard to certain matters specified in the Act. The grounds which a landlord may establish include breach by the tenant of certain of his obligations, that the landlord intends to demolish or reconstruct the premises, and that the landlord intends to occupy the premises himself (provided that the landlord's interest has not been purchased or created less than five years before the termination of the tenancy). If a new tenancy is refused on certain of these grounds, notably the last two that have been mentioned, the tenant is entitled to compensation. This compensation is equal to the rateable value of the premises, unless the tenant and his predecessors have occupied the premises for business purposes for the last 14 years, in which case the amount is twice the rateable value of the premises.

---

[37] s. 2 (1) (*a*).
[38] See p. 43, *ante.*
[39] See p. 39, *ante.*

There are certain exceptions to the Act, *e.g.* agricultural holdings, service tenancies, and " controlled tenancies " protected by the Rent Act 1968.

Under the Landlord and Tenant Act 1927 a tenant may recover compensation from his landlord for improvements which he has made to business premises if these have added to their letting value.

Agricultural holdings

Mention has already been made of some of the provisions of the Agricultural Holdings Act 1948, which give certain protection to the tenant of an agricultural holding.[40]

The Act also gives to a tenant who receives notice to quit from his landlord the right to serve a counter-notice upon the landlord, claiming the benefit of the Act, whereupon the notice to quit will become inoperative unless the agricultural land tribunal consents to its taking effect, which it can do only in five cases, *e.g.* in order to enable the landlord to carry out some purpose which is desirable in the interests of good husbandry. In certain cases, however, the tenant has no right to serve a counter-notice, *e.g.* where the landlord's interest in the holding has been materially prejudiced by an irreparable breach by the tenant of a term of the tenancy. (Any question as to whethere the tenant has a right to serve a counter-notice is settled by arbitration.)

A tenant who is required by his landlord to quit the land is (with some exceptions) entitled to compensation for disturbance. The amount of the compensation is not less than one and not more than two years' rent. A tenant who quits his holding is also entitled to compensation for certain improvements carried out by him. (There are detailed conditions which it is not proposed to set out here.) The amount of the compensation is generally the increase in the value of the holding, but where the improvement is of a short term character the amount is the value of the improvement to a new tenant.

There are also provisions under the Act by which from time to time either party may require the amount of the rent to be settled by arbitration.

---

[40] See p. 29, *ante.*

CHAPTER 11

CONTRACTS FOR THE DISPOSITION OF LAND

THE same substantive requirements apply to contracts to sell or otherwise dispose of land as to other contracts, but the Law of Property Act 1925, s. 40 (1), provides that " no action may be brought upon any contract for the sale or other disposition of land or any interest in land, unless the agreement upon which such action is brought, or some memorandum or note thereof, is in writing and signed by the party to be charged [*i.e.* the party sued] or by some other person thereunto by him lawfully authorised."

It is not necessary that the agreement itself should be in writing: all that is required is that before any action is brought to enforce it there shall be in existence some written document which is signed by the defendant and which sufficiently describes the subject-matter, identifies the parties, and states the consideration and other material terms of the agreement. No particular form is required, and it may be possible to spell out a sufficient memorandum from several documents (*e.g.* letters), one only of which is signed by the defendant, so long as on the face of them they are connected.[1] Even a document denying liability under the alleged contract will suffice, provided that it acknowledges that the contract exists; but it seems a document purporting to set out the terms of an agreement " subject to contract " (*i.e.* one which is not intended to be legally binding) cannot constitute a sufficient memorandum of an oral contract previously concluded in similar terms.[2]

If there is insufficient written evidence to satisfy the requirements of section 40 (1), neither party can enforce the contract by an action for damages. The contract is not void, however, and may be relied on, *e.g.* as a *defence* to an action by a defaulting purchaser to recover his deposit. More important, it may be enforced in equity by an action for specific performance, despite the lack of written evidence, provided that there are sufficient acts of part performance by the plaintiff. The equitable doctrine of part performance[3] is designed to prevent unfair advantage being taken of the absence of written evidence, where one party has allowed the other to act upon the faith of an agreement between them. The conditions for its application include the following.

---

[1] But see *Timmins* v. *Moreland Street Property Co. Ltd.* [1958] Ch. 110.
[2] *Tiverton Estates Ltd.* v. *Wearwell Ltd.* [1974] 2 W.L.R. 176, C.A., not following *Law* v. *Jones* [1974] Ch. 112, C.A., and doubting *Griffiths* v. *Young* [1970] 1 Ch. 675.
[3] The doctrine is recognised in s. 40 (2) of the Law of Property Act 1925.

First, the parties must have made a definite binding contract; secondly, the contract must be specifically enforceable [4]; thirdly, the acts relied upon must be those of the plaintiff and must be unequivocally referable to some contract of the kind alleged [5]: in most cases a change of possession is regarded as sufficient evidence of a contract of sale or of an agreement for a lease, *i.e.* entering into possession is generally a sufficient act of part-performance by the purchaser or tenant, and giving up possession is generally sufficient on the part of the vendor or landlord.

As has already been seen, the effect of a contract for the disposition of land, provided that it is evidenced by sufficient writing to comply with section 40 (1) of the Law of Property Act 1925, or by sufficient acts of part performance, is that not only can it be enforced by an action for damages or for specific performance, but also it is regarded in equity as at once giving rise to an equitable interest in the land.[6] The legal estate does not vest in the purchaser or lessee, however, until the formal conveyance or lease has been executed.

---

[4] The equitable remedy of specific performance is discretionary, and may be refused on a number of grounds, *e.g.* mistake, misrepresentation, undue delay, or breach of covenant (see *Warmington* v. *Miller* [1973] Q.B. 877).

[5] *Kingswood Estate Co. Ltd.* v. *Anderson* [1963] 2 Q.B. 169.

[6] See Chap. 5, *ante.*

CHAPTER 12

SETTLEMENTS

A SETTLEMENT of property is a disposition of property which creates a succession of interests in it, *e.g.* where property is settled on A for life with remainder to B in fee simple. Settlements of land are of two kinds, namely (i) the strict settlement,[1] which is governed by the Settled Land Act 1925, and (ii) the trust for sale, which is governed by the Law of Property Act 1925. The principal difference between the two is that under a strict settlement the legal estate, together with the powers of disposition over it, are and must be vested in the tenant for life (*i.e.*, broadly, the person who is for the time being beneficially entitled in possession under the terms of the settlement), whereas under a trust for sale it is the trustees who have both the legal estate and the powers of disposition.

The expression " settled land " means land which is subject to a strict settlement, and the broad effect of section 1 of the Settled Land Act is that land is settled land, and accordingly subject to the Act, wherever it is limited in trust for persons by way of succession or is subject to family charges (*e.g.* an annuity in favour of the settlor's widow).[2] Land which is held upon immediate binding trust for sale, however, is excluded from the operation of the Act. Such a trust for sale will normally be imposed expressly by the settlor, with the specific object of avoiding the provisions of the Settled Land Act; but in certain circumstances a trust for sale may also arise by statute.[3] It will be observed that the settlement will be a strict settlement governed by the Settled Land Act unless there is a trust for sale which is immediate and binding. A trust for sale is " immediate " if it is operative now and not merely in the future. Thus, if land is settled on A for life with remainder upon trust for sale for the benefit of B for life with remainders over (*i.e.* some further remainder or remainders), then during A's lifetime the land will be settled land and subject to the Settled Land Act, because the trust for sale is not immediate. When A dies, however, the trust for sale will become immediate and the land will cease to be settled land, and the Law of Property Act will then apply. The meaning of the word " binding " is a matter of

---

[1] The expression " settlement " is commonly used as referring to strict settlements only.

[2] The Act also applies where land is held in trust for a minor: see p. 120, *post.*

[3] There is a statutory trust for sale if two or more persons are entitled in possession in undivided shares (Settled Land Act 1925, s. 36). See Chap. 13.

doubt. Possibly it is merely a word of emphasis, designed to stress that land will be settled land unless there is a *trust* to sell it (*i.e.* an obligation to sell it), and that the mere fact that the instrument confers a *power* of sale will not take the settlement out of the Settled Land Act.[4]

The Law of Property Act 1925, s. 205, makes two points clear. A trust for sale which is otherwise immediate and binding is not prevented from being so by reason of the fact that the trustees are given power to postpone sale, or the fact that they are required to obtain the consents of specified persons before selling.

Strict Settlements

Vesting instrument and trust instrument

To create a strict settlement *inter vivos* the settlor must employ two documents, namely (i) the *vesting deed*, by which he transfers the land to the tenant for life, and (ii) the *trust instrument*, by which he declares the beneficial interests.[5] If the settlor himself is to be the tenant for life the vesting deed will declare that the land is vested in him.

If a strict settlement is created by will, the will ranks as the trust instrument, and the vesting deed is replaced by a vesting assent by which the testator's personal representatives transfer the land to the tenant for life.[6] (Personal representatives have the power to transfer land by a written instrument—it need not be under seal—called an " assent.")

The trust instrument must: (a) declare the trusts affecting the settled land; (b) appoint trustees of the settlement; (c) contain the power, if any, to appoint new trustees of the settlement; (d) set out any powers intended to be conferred by the settlement in extension of those conferred by the Act; and (e) bear any stamp duty which may be payable in respect of the settlement.[7]

The vesting deed or vesting assent must contain the following statements and particulars: (a) a description of the settled land; (b) a statement that the settled land is vested in the person or persons to whom it is conveyed, or in whom it is declared to be vested, upon the trusts from time to time affecting the settled land; (c) the names of the persons who are the trustees of the settlement; (d) any additional or larger powers conferred by the trust instrument; and (e) the name

---

[4] For other possible meanings, see Megarry and Wade's *Real Property*, 4th ed., 360–362 (3rd ed., 368–370).
[5] Settled Land Act 1925, s. 4.
[6] Settled Land Act 1925, ss. 6, 8
[7] *Ibid.* s. 4.

of any person for the time being entitled to appoint new trustees of the settlement.[8]

Tenant for life

The expression " tenant for life " is defined in detail in the Settled Land Act 1925, ss. 19 and 20, and means broadly any person of full age who is for the time being entitled in possession either to the land itself or to the income of the land (*e.g.* when the land is already leased to tenants).[9] It is irrelevant what the nature of his beneficial interest may be: whether he has a life interest itself, or an entailed interest, or a conditional or determinable fee, or even a fee simple or term of years absolute subject to family charges, he will be the tenant for life for the purposes of the Act, provided his interest is in possession.

It follows that only in rare cases will it happen that there is no person who satisfies the statutory definition of tenant for life. If, however, there is no such person,[10] or if there is but he is not of full age, the settled land and the statutory powers of disposition will be vested in the " statutory owner." This is defined [11] as the person of full age upon whom the settlement expressly confers the powers of a tenant for life, or, in any other case, the trustees of the settlement.

Powers of tenant for life

The statutory powers of a tenant for life are contained in Part II of the Settled Land Act 1925.

These powers may be enlarged by the express terms of the settlement,[12] and any powers which the settlement purports to confer on the trustees or on other persons will be regarded as additional powers of the tenant for life, and exercisable by him alone.[13]

The most important of the statutory powers are those of sale, leasing, and raising money on mortgage.

(a) *Power of sale*

The tenant for life may sell the settled land or any part thereof, or any easement, right or privilege of any kind over or in relation to the land.

---

[8] *Ibid.* s. 5.
[9] If two or more persons are jointly so entitled they together constitute the tenant for life.
[10] For examples, see *Re Frewen* [1926] Ch. 580; *Re Gallenga* [1938] 1 All E.R. 106.
[11] Settled Land Act 1925, ss. 23 (1), 117 (1) (xxvi). References throughout this chapter to the tenant for life should be taken as including the statutory owner, except where the context indicates the contrary.
[12] Settled Land Act 1925, s. 109.
[13] Settled Land Act 1925, s. 108.

(b) *Leasing powers*

The tenant for life may grant a building lease or a forestry lease [14] for a term not exceeding 999 years; a mining lease for a term not exceeding 100 years; and any other lease for a term not exceeding 50 years.

(c) *Power to mortgage*

The tenant for life may raise money by mortgage of the settled land for a number of purposes specified in section 71 of the Act, and in particular to pay for *improvements* authorised by the Act under provisions which we are now to consider.

(d) *Improvements*

The tenant for life may require capital money to be applied in payment for certain improvements, which are specified in the Third Schedule to the Act. This Schedule is divided into three parts. Part I contains a long list of improvements including the construction of drainage, farm roads and farm-houses and other farm buildings. In respect of these the tenant for life cannot be required to repay the cost. Part II contains a much shorter list which includes the building of dwelling-houses generally and the restoration or reconstruction of buildings damaged or destroyed by dry rot. In this case the trustees of the settlement may (and shall if so directed by the court) require that the money expended be repaid to them out of the income of the settled land by not more than 50 half-yearly instalments. Part III includes items such as the provision of heating, hydraulic or electric power apparatus for buildings, the installation of artificial light in any building, and the purchase of movable machinery for farming or other purposes. In this case the trustees of the settlement must require repayment by such instalments as have been mentioned.

Personal character of statutory powers

The powers conferred by the Act upon a tenant for life are personal to him and they remain with him notwithstanding any assignment of his beneficial interest, whether express or by operation of law, *e.g.* on his bankruptcy (when his beneficial interest would pass to his trustee in bankruptcy for the benefit of his creditors).[15]

An exception to this principle arises when a tenant for life, with intent to extinguish his beneficial interest, assigns it to the person next entitled in remainder or reversion under this settlement. The remainder is then accelerated and the tenant for life loses his statutory

---

[14] *i.e.* a lease granted to the Minister of Agriculture, Fisheries and Food.
[15] Settled Land Act 1925, s. 104, which also provides that any contract not to exercise the statutory powers shall be void.

powers.[16] For example, if land is settled on A for life with remainder to B for life, and A assigns his life interest to B (who is of full age) with intent to extinguish it, the remainder is accelerated, B becomes the tenant for life under the Settled Land Act, and A must by vesting deed convey the legal estate to him. Had the remainder to B been in fee simple the remainder again would have been accelerated and the settlement would have come to an end.

If a tenant for life has ceased (by reason of bankruptcy, assignment or otherwise) to have a substantial interest in the settled land, and either he has unreasonably refused to exercise any of his statutory powers, or he consents to an order, the court may make an order authorising the trustees of the settlement to exercise in the name and on behalf of the tenant for life any of the powers conferred upon him by the Act. To this extent the tenant for life is then precluded from exercising his powers.[17]

Protection of statutory powers

The Act invalidates any provision in a settlement which purports to exclude or restrict the powers conferred by the Act on a tenant for life: any provision in the settlement is void to the extent that it would even tend to prevent a tenant for life from exercising the powers.[18] For example, should the settlement provide that the tenant for life's interest shall come to an end if he ceases to reside on the settled land, this provision will be inoperative if the tenant for life sells or grants a lease of the land and for that reason ceases to reside on it (but the provision will become operative if the tenant for life ceases to reside on the land for a reason which is unconnected with his statutory powers). It follows that in the former case he will not forfeit his beneficial interest in the proceeds of sale or in the rents and profits of the land.[19]

The tenant for life as trustee

As we have seen, the legal estate in the land (*i.e.* the fee simple or, if the property settled is leasehold, the term of years) is vested in the tenant for life together with the statutory powers of disposition. The tenant for life is not the beneficial owner of the legal estate—if he was, there could be no settlement because there would be no succession of interests. He holds the legal estate upon trust for the beneficiaries in accordance with the terms of the trust instrument. A tenant for life, therefore, is in a dual position. Under the trust instrument he has whatever beneficial interest is conferred upon him,

---

[16] *Ibid.* s. 105.
[17] *Ibid.* s. 24.
[18] Settled Land Act 1925, s. 106.
[19] *Re Acklom* [1929] 1 Ch. 195.

e.g. a life interest or an entailed interest, and of this he is absolute owner. Under the vesting deed, or vesting assent, he has the entire legal estate, but this he holds as trustee.

The Act provides generally that a tenant for life shall, in exercising any power under the Act, have regard to the interests of all parties entitled under the settlement, and shall in relation to the exercise thereof by him be deemed to be in the position and to have the duties and liabilities of a trustee for those parties.[20] The tenant for life, however, is not as such a " trustee of the settlement." [21] The trustees of the settlement must be expressly appointed by the trust instrument, and they have distinct functions under the Act.

The tenant for life can make no disposition of the land except such as the Settled Land Act authorises him to make,[22] and although the Act does in fact give him wide powers of disposition, it attaches conditions which are designed to protect the interests of the other beneficiaries. Thus, in respect of most transactions he is required to give written notice to the trustees of the settlement; exceptionally, he may be required to obtain their consent or an order of the court.[23] Again, on a sale or lease of the settled land he must obtain the best consideration in money, or the best rent, that can reasonably be obtained. Above all, any capital money arising on a disposition of the settled land must be paid, not to the tenant for life, but to the trustees of the settlement, who will then hold it upon the same trusts as those affecting the land.

Dealings between the tenant for life and the estate

If special provision had not been made by the Act, the fiduciary position of the tenant for life would have precluded any dealing between himself and the estate: for example, it would not have been possible for him to purchase or take a lease of the settled land for his own benefit.

Of course he already holds his life or other interest beneficially, and by virtue of this is entitled to occupy the settled land or receive the rents and profits during his life; but it may happen that he wishes to acquire a more permanent interest, such as the fee simple or a long lease.

---

[20] Settled Land Act 1925, s. 107. The statutory powers, however, are discretionary, and his discretion whether or not to exercise them cannot ordinarily be challenged (*Re 90, Thornhill Road, Tolworth, Surrey* [1970] Ch. 261).
[21] There is nothing to prevent his being expressly appointed as a trustee of the settlement.
[22] s. 18.
[23] Notably with respect to dispositions of the principal mansion house (if the settlement expressly so requires), and the sale of settled chattels (which can only be sold under an order of the court). (Settled Land Act 1925, ss. 65, 67.)

Section 68 of the Act permits such dealings if a prescribed procedure is followed. The tenant for life must inform the trustees of the settlement of his wish, *e.g.* to purchase part of the settled land, and the trustees of the settlement then take over the powers of the tenant for life with regard to that transaction. They will decide whether the transaction should be permitted and, if they agree in principle, will negotiate the terms of the transaction with the tenant for life.

Overreaching

When the tenant for life sells the land, or any part of it, in exercise of his statutory power of sale the purchaser should pay his purchase money to the trustees of the settlement [24] and ensure that they are at least two in number or a trust corporation (*i.e.* a corporation authorised by law to undertake trust business).[25] If he does so he will acquire the land free from the interests of the beneficiaries under the settlement even though he knows of their existence.[26] But the beneficiaries are not prejudiced, because, as we have seen, the proceeds of sale are held by the trustees upon the same trusts as those upon which the land was held by the tenant for life before the sale. The interests of the beneficiaries, therefore, are said to be overreached, because they are taken away from the land and attached instead to the proceeds of sale. Any other disposition which the tenant for life is authorised by the Act to make, such as a lease, has a similar over-reaching effect.

As an illustration, suppose that land has been settled upon A for life, with remainder to B in fee simple, and that A is of full age. A is the tenant for life and the legal fee simple will have been vested in him by the vesting deed or vesting assent. Now suppose that in the exercise of his statutory power of sale A has sold half the settled land. The half that has not been sold remains vested in A and he holds it upon trust for himself for life with remainder to B in fee simple. The proceeds of sale of the other half will have been paid to the trustees of the settlement, and the purchaser accordingly will take the land free from the interests of A and B. The trustees normally will invest the proceeds in authorised trustee securities.[27] These securities will be registered in the names of the trustees of the settlement, who will hold them upon trust for A for life with remainder

---

[24] Or into court.

[25] Settled Land Act 1925, s. 18.

[26] *Ibid.* s. 72; Law of Property Act 1925, s. 2.

[27] See the Settled Land Act 1925, s. 73, for other authorised modes of applying capital money. These include the purchase of other land (freehold or a leasehold having 60 years or more to run), which will be brought into the settlement and conveyed to the tenant for life by subsidiary vesting deed.

to B in fee simple. (" In fee simple " is correct because capital money remains notionally land.[28])

In addition to beneficial interests subsisting or capable of arising under the settlement, a disposition by the tenant for life overreaches annuities, limited owner's charges, and general equitable charges (as those expressions are defined by the Land Charges Act 1972), even if created before the settlement and even if registered under the Land Charges Act. Suppose, for example, that S, the fee simple owner of Blackacre, creates an equitable mortgage of the land which is not protected by deposit of title deeds with the mortgagee, and that this mortgage (which is a general equitable charge) is registered under the Land Charges Act. Suppose that afterwards S settles the land on A for life with remainder to B in fee simple and that A sells the land under his statutory power of sale as tenant for life, the purchaser will acquire the land free from the equitable mortgage as well as the rights of the beneficiaries under the settlement. The mortgagee is not prejudiced, however, and can claim payment from the trustees of the settlement—his mortgage is overreached, not extinguished.

The " curtain " principle

On a sale, lease, mortgage or other disposition of settled land, a purchaser dealing in good faith with the tenant for life is conclusively taken to have given the best price, consideration or rent that could reasonably be obtained, and to have complied with all the requisitions of the Act.[29]

The purchaser is neither bound nor entitled to inspect the trust instrument [30] : this relates to interests which will be overreached by the conveyance to him and he is therefore in no way concerned with it. It is therefore said to be " behind the curtain " (hidden from him) as regards the purchaser. On the other hand, he is very much concerned with the vesting deed or vesting assent, which is designed to give him the information that he requires, including the names of the trustees of the settlement, to whom he must pay his purchase money, and he is, in general, required to assume the accuracy of the statements in this instrument.[31] There are certain exceptions to these rules, of which the most important are subsisting settlements created before 1926 and imperfectly constituted post-1925 settlements.

---

[28] Settled Land Act 1925, s. 75.
[29] Settled Land Act 1925, s. 110 (1). The relation between this provision and s. 18 (which makes *void* any unauthorised disposition: see p. 53, *ante*) is uncertain (*cf. Weston* v. *Henshaw* [1950] Ch. 510, *Re Morgan's Lease* [1972] Ch. 1).
[30] *Ibid.* s. 110 (2).
[31] Settled Land Act 1925, s. 110 (2).

Duration of settlement

Once a settlement comes into operation the land remains settled land so long as any beneficial interest under the settlement subsists or is capable of arising or the beneficial owner is an infant.[32] Suppose, for example, that land is settled on A for life with remainder to B in fee simple, but subject to a jointure rentcharge for A's widow (*i.e.* subject to a charge upon the land for payment of an annual sum to A's widow during her widowhood). Upon the death of A, leaving a widow, the land remains settled land because it is still subject to the charge, and B, if of full age, is the tenant for life. If B, as tenant for life, sells the land under his statutory power of sale, the widow's jointure will be overreached. The widow will not be prejudiced, however, because the proceeds of sale will be paid to the trustees of the settlement, who will be responsible for payment to the widow of her jointure. Alternatively, in this particular case, when the land is settled land by reason only that it is subject to such a charge for the payment of money, the Law of Property (Amendment) Act 1926 allows B to sell the land subject to the charge as if it were not settled land and himself receive the proceeds of sale—if this procedure is adopted the purchase money will, of course, be less, because the purchaser will acquire the land saddled with the burden of paying the jointure to the widow.

Death of tenant for life

If on the death of a tenant for life the land remains settled land, the trustees of the settlement are entitled to a grant of probate (if the tenant for life died testate) or letters of administration, limited to the settled land. They then become his special personal representatives with regard to the settled land,[33] and must vest the settled land in the next tenant for life.[34] On the other hand, if when a tenant for life dies the land ceases to be settled land, the land will devolve upon the tenant for life's general (*i.e.* ordinary) personal representatives,[35] who will vest it in the person or persons entitled to it. For example, if land is settled on A for life with remainder to B for life with remainder to C in fee simple and A, B and C are of full age, then on the death of A the settled land will devolve upon A's special personal representatives. They will vest the land in B, the next tenant for life, by means of a vesting assent.[36] But when B dies the land will cease to be settled land. It will therefore devolve upon B's general personal

---

[32] Settled Land Act 1925, s. 3.
[33] Administration of Estates Act 1925, s. 22.
[34] Settled Land Act 1925, s. 7.
[35] *Re Bridgett and Hayes' Contract* [1928] Ch. 163.
[36] Settled Land Act 1925, s. 8.

representatives and they will vest it in C by a simple written assent
(a vesting assent, containing the same particulars as a vesting deed,
will not be appropriate as the land will have ceased to be settled
land).

Deed of discharge

When a settlement comes to an end the trustees of the settlement
may be required to execute a deed of discharge, i.e. a deed declaring
that they are discharged from the trusts of the settlement. In the event
of any difficulty the court may be asked to make an order of discharge
which will have the same effect. Unless the deed or order of discharge
states the contrary (e.g. it indicates that the land it still settled land
under a derivative settlement) a purchaser of the land will be entitled
to assume that the land has ceased to be settled land and is not subject
to a trust for sale.[37]

Such a deed or order of discharge is not necessary if land which
was formerly settled land has been disposed of by an ordinary deed
of conveyance or a simple written assent, because a purchaser is
then bound and entitled to act on the assumption that the settlement
has come to an end, at any rate as regards that land.[38] For example,
as we have seen, if on the death of a tenant for life the land ceases
to be settled land the land will devolve upon his ordinary personal
representatives, and they will vest the land in the person or persons
entitled to it by a simple written assent. A subsequent purchaser
upon investigating the title to the land will see that it has been disposed of by this simple written assent, and he will then be bound
and entitled to assume that the land in question has ceased to be
settled land. This point is of importance because if land is settled
land a purchaser must pay his purchase money to the trustees of the
settlement (or into court).[39]

Trusts for Sale

Trusts for sale are not solely employed as a method of creating settlements of land outside the provisions of the Settled Land Act. They are
equally important in the context of two quite different situations
where a trust for sale is imposed by statute, namely co-ownership
(under the Law of Property Act 1925, ss. 34–36) and intestacy (under
the Administration of Estates Act 1925, s. 33).[40]

Technically a trust for sale of land is not a settlement of land, but

---

[37] Ibid. s. 17.
[38] Ibid. s. 110 (5).
[39] See p. 54, ante.
[40] See Chaps. 13 and 25 respectively. The general discussion of trusts for
sale in the present chapter should be taken as applying equally to statutory
trusts for sale.

of money, by reason of the equitable doctrine of conversion, which in
turn is based on the maxim " equity looks upon that as done which
ought to be done." As the trustees are bound to sell the land equity
looks upon that as done, *i.e.* upon the land as having already been
sold, and this is so even if the trustees have the usual power to postpone sale (trustees for sale of land always have power to postpone the
sale unless the trust instrument otherwise provides).[41] The interests of
the beneficiaries under a trust for sale, therefore, are in theory interests
in money from the beginning.[42]

To create a trust for sale *inter vivos* the settlor conveys the land
to trustees upon trust to sell it and to hold the net rents and profits
pending sale and the proceeds of sale after sale upon trust for certain
beneficiaries, *e.g.* on trust for A for life with remainder to B absolutely. The trustees then have the legal estate in the land (*i.e.* the
legal fee simple or if a leasehold is settled the legal term of years)
and the beneficiaries have interests in the proceeds of sale. Thus, in
the example given A has the right to receive the net rents and profits
of the land pending sale and the income from the investments of
the proceeds of sale after sale. Upon the death of A, if the land
has not been sold, B will be entitled to require the trustees to convey
the land to him; if the land has been sold B will be entitled to require
the trustees to transfer to him the investments made with the proceeds
of sale. Both the conveyance of the land to the trustees and the declaration of the trusts can be done in one document; there is no two-
document rule as in the case of strict settlements. But except in simple
cases it is good conveyancing practice to employ two documents,
namely (i) a conveyance upon trust for sale and (ii) a separate trust
instrument. If this is done, the conveyance transfers the land and
imposes the trust to sell it, but does not set out the beneficial interests:
these are set out in the trust instrument. The " curtain " principle then
operates, *i.e.* a purchaser of the land from the trustees is not concerned with the trust instrument.

When land is given by will upon trust for sale there are normally
two documents. The testator's personal representatives will transfer
the land to the trustees by a written " assent upon trust for sale."
This assent will then correspond to the conveyance upon trust for
sale and will not declare the beneficial interests. The will itself operates
as the trust instrument: it must be referred to in order to ascertain
what the beneficial interests are, but so far as a purchaser is concerned it is " behind the curtain." [43]

---

[41] Law of Property Act 1925, s. 25.
[42] It follows, at least where a trust for sale is created expressly, that the
beneficiaries may not be entitled to possession of the land itself (*Barclay* v.
Barclay [1970] 2 Q.B. 677; contrast *Bull* v. *Bull* [1955] 1 Q.B. 234, C.A.).
[43] Administration of Estates Act 1925, s. 36.

A purchaser from the trustees will naturally pay his purchase money to the trustees, and he should ensure that they are at least two in number or a trust corporation. The purchaser will not then be concerned with the trusts affecting the proceeds of sale [44]; in effect this means that the beneficial interests will be overreached, although strictly the case is not one of overreaching because, by reason of the equitable doctrine of conversion, the interests of the beneficiaries are in theory interests in the proceeds of sale of the land from the beginning.

As we have seen, trustees for sale have power to postpone sale. However, this power to postpone sale can be exercised only so long as the trustees are unanimously agreed to do so. In the absence of special circumstances, therefore, any trustee can insist upon an immediate sale.[45] This rule may be excluded in particular circumstances, e.g. where the trustees are also the beneficial owners and for one of them to insist upon an immediate sale would be contrary to some express or implied agreement between them.

If the instrument which creates a trust for sale requires the trustees to obtain the consent of more than two persons before selling, then in favour of a purchaser the consent of any two of such persons shall be sufficient. (It would seem, however, that the trustees would commit a breach of trust if they did not obtain the consent of all the persons specified, although the title of the purchaser to the land would not be affected by that failure.) The Act also provides that where a person whose consent is required is under disability his consent shall not, in favour of a purchaser, be deemed to be requisite; but the trustees shall in any such case obtain the separate consent of the parent or guardian of an infant or the receiver (if any) of a person suffering from mental disorder.[46]

Powers of trustees for sale

The Law of Property Act 1925, s. 28, provides that trustees for sale shall, in relation to land and to the proceeds of sale, have all the powers of a tenant for life and the trustees of a settlement under the Settled Land Act 1925. (Before exercising any such power, however, the trustees must obtain the same consents, if any, as would have been required on a sale of the land.) The trustees, for example, will have the same powers of granting leases of the land as a tenant for life would have had, and the same powers of investment as the trustees of the settlement would have had, if the land had been settled land.

One of the consequences of this provision is that trustees for sale

---

[44] Law of Property Act 1925, s. 27.
[45] *Re Mayo* [1943] Ch. 302.
[46] Law of Property Act 1925, s. 26.

who have sold part of their land may use the proceeds of sale for
the purchase of other land, being freehold or a leasehold having at
least 60 years to run.[47] Any such land will be conveyed to the trustees
and will be held by them upon trust for sale.[48] It has been held that
once trustees for sale have sold all their land they no longer possess
this power, being no longer within the terms of section 28, and therefore have no power to buy land unless such a power is conferred
upon them by the terms of the settlement.[49]

Another consequence of the provision is that capital money held
by trustees for sale may be applied to payment for improvements to
land still held by them in the same way that capital money under the
Settled Land Act may be used for paying for improvements.[50]
Trustees for sale always have power to pay for the cost of repairs out
of income. It will sometimes happen that a particular repair is also
an improvement within the Settled Land Act, or some other improvement of a permanent nature,[51] in which case the trustees will have a
discretion as to whether that repair shall be paid for out of income
or out of capital.

Delegation

Trustees for sale of land may by writing revocably delegate from
time to time their powers of leasing, accepting surrenders of leases, and
management to any person of full age (not being merely an annuitant)
for the time being beneficially entitled in possession to the net rents
and profits of the land during his life or for any less period.[52]

Powers of the court

The Law of Property Act 1925, s. 30, provides that if trustees for sale
refuse to sell or exercise any of their statutory powers of disposition,
or to make such delegation as has just been mentioned, the court
may direct them to do so; and if any requisite consent cannot be
obtained the court may dispense with it. The court is thus enabled to
exercise over trusts for sale a measure of control which is signally
lacking with respect to settlements taking effect under the Settled
Land Act.[53]

Special (or Ad Hoc) Trusts for Sale and Ad Hoc Settlements

If the trustees of a trust for sale are either (i) two or more persons
approved or appointed by the court, or their successors in office, or
(ii) a trust corporation, a conveyance by the trustees to a purchaser

---

[47] See *Re Wellsted's Will Trusts* [1949] Ch. 296, C.A.
[48] Law of Property Act 1925, s. 28.   [49] *Re Wakeman* [1945] Ch. 177.
[50] Law of Property Act 1925, s. 28.
[51] *Re Smith* [1930] 1 Ch. 88.
[52] Law of Property Act 1925, s. 29.   [53] See p. 53, note 20, *ante*.

has a somewhat wider overreaching effect than would otherwise be the case. Certain equitable interests having priority to the trust for sale can be overreached which could not have been overreached if the trust for sale had not been in this special category.[54] A trust for sale may be specially set up in order that a contemplated sale of the land shall have this wider overreaching effect, in which case the trust for sale may be called an *ad hoc* trust for sale.

Very similarly, an estate owner may set up an *ad hoc* settlement under the Settled Land Act 1925, for the express purpose of over-reaching equitable interests which could not otherwise have been overreached. The trustees of the settlement must then be two or more persons approved or appointed by the court or a trust corporation.[55]

These provisions of the Law of Property Act 1925 and the Settled Land Act 1925 are little used and are relatively unimportant. Their detail need not detain us.

Settlements Old and New

Traditionally, the typical settlement was a marriage settlement. If it was desired to keep the land in the family as far as possible, a strict settlement was used, whereas if the land was regarded as an investment a trust for sale was employed (and the settlement was then often known as a trader's settlement).

Assuming that the land was brought into the settlement by the husband and that a strict settlement was used, the husband would settle the land on himself for life with remainder to his first and other sons successively in order of seniority in tail. Subsidiary provision would also be made for the wife, both during the marriage and during widowhood, and for any younger sons and daughters of the marriage. When the eldest son came of age, his father would induce him to bar the entail with his consent, thereby converting the fee tail into a full fee simple. This fee simple would then be resettled on the son for life with remainder to *his* sons in tail. The result would be that when the father died and the son came into possession of the land he would do so as a mere tenant for life. This process of re-settlement would be repeated generation by generation, and in consequence the tenant in possession of the land at any given time would have only a life estate and no power to dispose of the land in fee simple. So undesirable were the social and economic consequences of this device for keeping the land in the same family that Parliament felt compelled to intervene and finally, by the Settled Land Act 1882, adopted the drastic solution of conferring upon the tenant for life a statutory power to sell the land or any part of it which no provision in the settlement

[54] *Ibid.* s. 2.
[55] Settled Land Act 1925, s. 21.

could exclude or restrict. This provision has been re-enacted by the Settled Land Act 1925,[56] and in consequence the use of a strict settlement does not ensure that the land will be kept in the family for even one generation.

If a marriage settlement was made by the husband by means of a trust for sale, the essential trusts would be for the husband for life with the remainder to the wife for life if she survived him, with remainder to the children or remoter issue of the marriage in such shares as the husband and wife should jointly by deed appoint and, in default of such appointment, as the survivor should by deed or will appoint and, in default for such of the children of the marriage as should attain the age of 21 or being females marry under that age.

Having regard to the historical difference between the strict settlement and the trust for sale, it is odd that today it is possible by means of the trust for sale to ensure that land is kept in the family at least for a time, whereas this is not possible if a strict settlement is employed. When a strict settlement is used no restriction can be imposed upon the statutory power of sale which is given to the tenant for life, but when a trust for sale is employed the trustees can be required to obtain the consents of specified persons before selling.[57]

By reason of the complicated conveyancing machinery which they involve, especially on the death of a tenant for life, strict settlements are little used today. Such a settlement may, however, be created inadvertently, e.g. when a testator by a home-made will leaves his house to his wife for her life and then to his children absolutely.[58] In recent times even the trust for sale in its traditional marriage settlement form has, for fiscal reasons, become increasingly rare. For example, in general if a trust creates a succession of beneficial interests, death duties become payable upon the full capital value of the trust property whenever the equitable interest passes on death from one beneficiary to another. If property is settled on, say, A for life with remainder to B for life with remainder to C absolutely, death duties become payable upon the deaths of A and B (if they die in that order), as well as upon the death of C if he is still the owner of the property when he dies. Strangely enough, in the hands of counsel or a solicitor with an expert knowledge of revenue law, trusts of a very different kind can be used as a means of *minimising* the burden of income tax and estate duty, and this is perhaps the most important use to which trusts are put by the lawyer today. Tax planning or tax avoidance (but never " evasion "), as it is somewhat euphemistically called, is beyond the scope of this book.

---

[56] s. 106, p. 52, *ante.*   [57] See p. 59, *ante.*
[58] For a more remote example of a settlement arising by inadvertence, see *Binions* v. *Evans* [1972] Ch. 359, C.A.

CHAPTER 13

CO-OWNERSHIP

CO-OWNERSHIP subsists when two or more persons have concurrent (not consecutive) interests in the same property. For example, if land is granted to A and B in fee simple, A and B are co-owners, but if land is settled on A for life with remainder to B in fee simple, A and B are not co-owners.

The main forms of co-ownership are joint tenancy and tenancy in common. The principal difference between the two is that the right of survivorship (or *jus accrescendi*) applies to joint tenancy, but not to tenancy in common. Thus, if A, B and C are joint tenants in fee simple and A dies, A's interest survives to B and C, who become owners of the whole. If B then dies his interest likewise survives to C, who becomes sole owner of the land: co-ownership is then at an end. It follows that a joint tenant has nothing which he can leave by his will or which will pass to his statutory next of kin if he dies intestate. But if A, B and C are tenants in common in fee simple and A dies, his interest does not survive to the others, but devolves upon his personal representatives and forms part of his estate.

The only other form of co-ownership which can subsist today is co-parcenary. This arises when under the old realty canons of descent land devolves upon two or more persons as co-heirs; hence after 1925 co-parcenary can only arise in those exceptional cases, such as the devolution of an unbarred entail, in which the old canons of descent still apply.[1] Today for all practical purposes co-parcenary is indistinguishable from tenancy in common, and it will not be necessary to refer to it again hereafter, except to mention that the expression " tenancy in undivided shares " embraces both tenancy in common and co-parcenary; this expression may be used therefore when it is desired to refer to those forms of co-ownership to which the right of survivorship does not apply.

Statutory trust for sale

After 1925, with one exception, whenever a disposition of land (by deed or by will) creates beneficial co-ownership in possession, whether it be joint tenancy or tenancy in common, the land is held upon statutory trust for sale.[2] The trustees are then said to hold the land

---

[1] See Chap. 25.
[2] The main provisions are in the Law of Property Act 1925, ss. 34–36. For some doubts that arise on the provisions see Megarry and Wade's *Real Property*, 4th ed., pp. 411–412 (3rd ed., pp. 423–424), and *Bull* v. *Bull* [1955] 1 Q.B. 234, C.A.

upon the " statutory trusts," *i.e.* upon trust to sell it and to hold the net rents and profits pending sale, and the proceeds of sale after sale, upon trust for the beneficial co-owners according to their interests. It will be observed that the statutory trust for sale does not apply to the land unless the co-ownership is in possession. If, therefore, land is settled on A for life, with remainder to B and C in fee simple, the land will be settled land under the Settled Land Act 1925, so long as A is alive; upon the death of A, however, the co-ownership will be in possession and a statutory trust for sale will then apply to the land.

The one exception to the general rule is that if land is settled on two or more *joint* tenants for life (and no express trust for sale is imposed) the land will be settled land under the Settled Land Act 1925, and the joint tenants for life (or those of them who are of full age) will together constitute the " tenant for life " of the Settled Land Act.[3] It may be noticed that, since in this case there is no *trust* for sale, but merely the *power* of sale conferred by the Act upon a tenant for life, no joint tenant for life can insist on the land being sold.[4]

The trustees of the trust for sale

The trustees of the statutory trust for sale are normally the beneficial co-owners themselves who are of full age or, if there are more than four such, then the first four named. There is an exception, however, when land is given by will to two or more persons as tenants in common. In this case the trustees of the trust for sale are the trustees of the will, if any, for the purposes of the Settled Land Act, or if none, the testator's personal representatives.

Now trustees have always been joint tenants. It follows that, even if the deed or will creates beneficial tenancy in common, the *legal estate* will be held jointly. Indeed, section 1 of the Law of Property Act 1925 expressly provides that after 1925 tenancy in common cannot subsist in respect of the legal estate. The purpose of this provision, and the reason why a trust for sale is imposed by sections 34 and 36 of the Law of Property Act 1925, is to facilitate dispositions of the legal estate. If before 1926 a legal estate in land was held by A, B and C as tenants in common, it might be disposed of without difficulty so long as all of them were alive; but if each died, leaving his share to (say) his four children, the land would now belong equally to twelve persons, all of whom had to join in a conveyance to a purchaser if the land was to be sold. Such difficulties cannot now arise, since a legal estate can only be held *jointly*, by not more than four trustees, and remains vested in the surviving trustees upon the death of any of

---

[3] Settled Land Act 1925, s. 19.
[4] *Re 90 Thornhill Road, Tolworth, Surrey* [1970] Ch. 261. Contrast *Re Mayo*, p. 59, *ante*.

them. A sale by the trustees will overreach [5] the beneficial interests subsisting under the trust whether they are held jointly or in common, and however diverse they may be. A few illustrations may help.

(i) Land is conveyed by deed to A, B and C (who are all of full age) as tenants in common in fee simple. The land passes to A, B and C as joint tenants in fee simple upon the statutory trusts for the benefit of themselves as tenants in common in equity (*i.e.* as beneficiaries under the trust for sale). If A then dies, the right of survivorship will operate with regard to the joint tenancy of the legal estate and the legal fee simple will become vested in B and C, the surviving trustees of the trust for sale, but A's beneficial (or equitable) interest as tenant in common will pass to his personal representatives and will form part of his estate.

(ii) If land is granted to A, B and C as joint tenants in fee simple, and A and B are of full age, but C is an infant, the land will pass to A and B as joint tenants upon the statutory trusts for the benefit of themselves and C as joint tenants in equity (*i.e.* as beneficiaries under the trust for sale). If A then dies, B will become the sole surviving trustee (and a further trustee should be appointed to act with him before a sale of the land is made).[6]

(iii) If land is conveyed by deed to A and B (both of whom are of full age) as joint tenants in fee simple, the land will pass to A and B as joint tenants upon the statutory trusts for themselves as joint tenants in equity. If A dies, and the joint tenancy under the trust for sale has not been converted into tenancy in common, B will become the sole owner at law and in equity. The trust for sale will then be at an end and B will be entitled to sell the land without the necessity of having an additional trustee appointed to act with him.[7]

(iv) Land is given by will to A and B as tenants in common in fee simple. Upon the testator's death the land will devolve upon his personal representatives. By written assent they will vest the land in the trustees of the statutory trust for sale. These trustees will be the trustees of the will for the purposes of the Settled Land Act 1925, if the will happens to appoint such trustees, and otherwise will be the personal representatives themselves. These trustees will hold the land upon the statutory trusts for the benefit of A and B as tenants in common in equity.

Joint tenancy or tenancy in common?

As we have seen, after 1925 there cannot be tenancy in common

---

[5] See Chap. 12 under *Trusts for sale.*
[6] *Ibid.*
[7] Law of Property (Amendment) Act 1926, Sched.; *Re Cook* [1948] Ch. 212. The Law of Property (Joint Tenants) Act 1964 facilitates proof of title by the survivor in such a case.

in relation to the legal estate, but the equitable interest under the trust for sale may be held jointly or in common. In order to ascertain whether it is one or the other in a given case it may be necessary to ask three questions.

(i) *Are the four unities present?* The four unities are those of possession, interest, title and time. The unity of possession means that each co-owner has possession of the whole; none can lay claim to separate ownership of any particular part of the property. The unity of interest means that each co-owner has the same interest both in quantity and in quality. Thus if one co-owner has a three-quarters interest and the other a one-quarter interest, this unity is lacking. Similarly, if one has a life interest and the other a fee simple interest, the unity is lacking. The unity of title means that each co-owner derives his title from the same document. The unity of time means that the interest of each co-owner has vested at the same time.

The unity of possession is essential to any form of co-ownership. The other three unities are essential to joint tenancy, but not to tenancy in common. If, therefore, one of these three unities is found to be lacking, it is not necessary to look further: the beneficial co-ownership is in common and not joint. But if these three unities are present, the beneficial co-ownership may be joint or in common, and it is necessary to ask the second question.

(ii) *Have words of severance been used in the grant?* Words of severance, such as " equally " or " in equal shares " or " share and share alike," are words which show an intention that each co-owner is to have a distinct share. If such words have been used the beneficial co-ownership is in common, but if no such words have been used the position remains uncertain and it will be necessary to ask the third question (unless indeed the document creating the co-ownership has expressly provided that it is to be joint).

(iii) *Is there any other indication of an intention to create tenancy in common?* It may be that the instrument as a whole will sufficiently show an intention to create tenancy in common, even though words of severance have not been used in the grant. Alternatively, in certain circumstances equity presumes an intention to create tenancy in common in the absence of sufficient evidence to the contrary. These cases are:

(i) When the co-owners have purchased the property and put up the purchase money in unequal proportions; the presumption is then that they intend to have interests in the property proportionate to their contributions.

(ii) When the co-owners are mortgagees, having taken the property as security for a loan which they have made; in this case it is immaterial whether they have advanced the loan money equally or unequally.

(iii) When the co-owners are partners and hold the property as part of their partnership assets.

In the absence of sufficient evidence of an intention to create tenancy in common, and if equity does not presume such an intention in the circumstances, the beneficial co-ownership will be joint.

Determination of co-ownership

Co-ownership may come to an end for any of the following reasons:

(i) *Partition*. Partition is a division of the land amongst those who are beneficially entitled under the statutory trust for sale. Obviously this can be effected if all those who are beneficially entitled are of full age and desire it. Provision is also made by statute for the trustees of the statutory trust for sale if they think fit to give their consent to partition on behalf of an infant beneficiary. Moreover, the court on application may direct a partition if it thinks fit.[8]

(ii) *Union*. One person may become solely entitled to the whole beneficial interest, *e.g.* one beneficiary under the statutory trust for sale may buy the interests of the others. The beneficial co-ownership will then be at an end.

(iii) *Severance*. Severance is a process by which joint tenancy can be converted into tenancy in common: co-ownership remains, but its character has been altered. After 1925 such a severance is, of course, possible only with regard to the beneficial interest under the statutory trust for sale, because there cannot be tenancy in common in relation to the legal estate. Severance may be effected by destroying either the unity of title or that of interest, both of which, as we have seen, are essential to joint tenancy. Thus if A, B and C are joint tenants in fee simple of the beneficial interest and A assigns his interest to D, D will become tenant in common as between himself and the others, who will remain joint tenants *inter se*; there is no unity of title between D, on the one hand, and B and C on the other. Again, if A, B and C are joint tenants for life and A acquires the fee simple in remainder or in reversion, A will become tenant in common as between himself and B and C; there is no unity of interest between A, on the one hand, and B and C on the other. It must, however, be noticed that if one of several joint tenants acquires the interest of another, so that his interest becomes greater merely in quantum than that of the others, severance occurs with regard only to the interest so acquired. For example, if A, B, C and D are joint tenants in fee simple of the beneficial interest and A acquires the interest of B, A will become

---

[8] Law of Property Act 1925, ss. 28, 30.

tenant in common as between himself and C and D with regard only
to the interest which he has acquired from B; he will remain joint
tenant in relation to his original interest.

Section 36 of the Law of Property Act 1925 has introduced an
additional method of severance by which a joint tenant may give a
written notice of severance to the others. This provision does not,
however, apply to joint tenants for life of settled land.

CHAPTER 14

THE PERPETUITY RULE

THE judges have always striven to prevent property owners, and in particular, land owners, from tying up their property by means of settlements for an excessive length of time. To a considerable extent this is also controlled by legislation, such as the Settled Land Act 1925, which as we have seen greatly facilitates dispositions of the legal estate in land that is subject to a settlement. Equally, however, it is the policy of the law to limit the extent to which equitable or beneficial interests in land or its proceeds or income may be tied up. Two weapons which the judges invented for this purpose were known as the old and the modern perpetuity rules, both of which existed in 1925. The Law of Property Act 1925 abolished the old rule, leaving us with only the modern rule to consider. It is called the modern rule in order to distinguish it from the other rule, but in fact it is a rule of some antiquity. It has been substantially modified by the Perpetuities and Accumulations Act 1964; but it will first be considered without reference to that Act.

The first point to notice about the rule is that it applies only to contingent interests in property. An interest is contingent for this purpose so long as the identity of the beneficiary in question is unknown and so long as any condition which has been annexed to the grant of his interest remains unfulfilled. Thus, if property is given to the first son of A to attain 21, and when the grant comes into operation no son has attained 21, the interest given to the son is contingent; the identity of the first son to attain 21 is unknown. Again, if property is given to John Brown if and when he attains the age of 21, and he has not already attained 21 when the grant comes into operation, John Brown's interest is contingent; a condition has been attached to his interest which has not yet been fulfilled.

The law allows a certain period for the vesting of a contingent interest and this period is known as the " perpetuity period." The perpetuity period is the lives of any persons referred to in the grant (expressly or by implication) who are living or conceived when the grant comes into operation, plus a further period of 21 years. The lives of *any* persons who are living or conceived when the grant comes into operation may be taken for this purpose provided that those persons are referred to in the grant expressly or by implication; they need not be beneficiaries. A few examples should make the position clear, but in the meantime the rule itself must now be stated.[1]

---

[1] In its present form the rule was finally settled in *Cadell* v. *Palmer* (1833) 1 Cl. & Fin. 372.

The rule is that a contingent interest is void if it might possibly vest after the end of the perpetuity period. In other words a contingent interest is void unless it is certain when the grant comes into operation that the interest *will* vest before the end of the permitted period, if indeed it vests at all (it is always possible that a contingent interest will not vest at all, but this is not a material consideration for the purposes of the rule). " Vest " simply means " cease to be contingent." We may now consider a few examples.

(i) Property is given to A (who is a bachelor when the grant comes into operation) for life with remainder to his first son to attain 21 absolutely. The remainder to the son is contingent because his identity is unknown when the grant comes into operation. The question, therefore, is whether this interest might possibly vest after the end of the permitted period (lives of persons in being [2] when the grant came into operation, plus a further period of 21 years). The answer is " no," and the remainder does not infringe the rule. A is living when the grant comes into operation and any son of his who attains 21 is bound to do so within 21 years after the death of A. Of course the remainder will fail if as events turn out no son of A attains 21, but that is a different matter: the remainder does not infringe the perpetuity rule—had it done so it would have been void *ab initio*.

(ii) A more difficult illustration. A testator leaves property to his first grandson to attain 21. When the will comes into operation on the testator's death no grandson has attained 21. The interest is contingent, because the beneficiary's identity is unknown. However, any grandson who attains 21 must do so within 21 years of the deaths of the testator's children, who are living when the grant comes into operation, and the interest is valid. This illustration shows that the lives of persons who are not beneficiaries (*i.e.* in this illustration the lives of the testator's children) may be considered for the purposes of the rule if those persons are living when the grant comes into operation.

(iii) A testator directs that his property shall be divided amongst all his descendants living at the death of the survivor of the descendants of his late Majesty King George VI who are living at the testator's death. In this case it is clear that by the very words of the gift the identities of the testator's descendants who will take the property will be known by the end of the lives of persons who are living when the grant comes into operation. Indeed the testator might have postponed the vesting for a further 21 years. In this type of case the only rule is that it must be practically possible to ascertain when the specified

---

[2] This expression may conveniently be used for " living or conceived " (or living or *en ventre sa mère*). The expression " lives of persons in being " may be further shortened to " lives in being."

lives come to an end.[3] Hence it would be foolish for a draftsman today to specify the lives of the descendants of Queen Victoria living when the grant came into operation.

(iv) Property is given to A (a bachelor) for life, with remainder to his first grandson to attain 21 absolutely. The remainder is void. The only person who is living when the grant comes into operation and who is referred to, expressly or by implication, in the grant is A. There is no certainty that the identity of the first grandson to attain 21 will be known within the life of A plus a further period of 21 years. It will make no difference if as events turn out a grandson of A does attain 21 within this period. An interest is void *ab initio* if it might possibly vest after the end of the permitted period. This rule is sometimes known as the rule that in the application of the perpetuity rule there is no " wait and see."

Statutory relief before the Act of 1964

The commonest cause in practice of infringement of the perpetuity rule is making the interest of a beneficiary contingent upon the attainment of an age greater than 21. However, the Law of Property Act 1925, s. 163, provides that if the interest of a beneficiary or beneficiaries is made contingent upon the attainment by the beneficiary or beneficiaries of an age greater than 21, and for that reason the interest would be void for remoteness, the age of 21 is to be substituted for that greater age. For example, if property is given to A (a bachelor) for life, with remainder to his first son to attain the age of 30 absolutely, the remainder is void as it stands, but section 163 substitutes the age of 21 for the offending age of 30, thereby validating the interest.

Two points must be noticed. First the section does not apply if an interest is valid as it stands. For example, if property is given to John Brown contingently on his attaining the age of 30, and John Brown has not attained that age when the grant comes into operation, the section has no application. John Brown is living when the grant comes into operation and he is bound to attain the age of 30, if at all, during his own life time. As it stands, therefore, the grant does not infringe the rule. Secondly, the section applies only when an interest is made contingent upon the attainment by the beneficiary or beneficiaries of an age greater than 21. Hence if a testator leaves property to be divided amongst all his descendants (living at, or born after, his death) who shall be living 30 years after his death, the section has no application and the gift is void.

Class gifts

A class gift is a gift to a class of persons by description, the mem-

---

[3] *Re Villar* [1929] 1 Ch. 243.

bers of which are not immediately ascertainable when the grant comes
into operation. For the purposes of the perpetuity rule a class gift is
wholly contingent until the identity of every possible member of the
class is known. Such a gift, therefore, is wholly void if when the grant
comes into operation there is any possibility that it may be necessary
to wait longer than the permitted period before the identity of every
possible member of the class is known. For example, if a testator
gives property to be divided amongst all A's grandchildren (whether
born at the testator's death or born thereafter),[4] and A is alive when
the will comes into operation, the gift is wholly void. Even grandchildren of A who are living at the date of the testator's death will
take nothing. Under the perpetuity rule a class gift must be wholly
valid or wholly void.[5]

Following remainders

If an interest infringes the perpetuity rule, a following remainder
will not thereby be invalidated unless it is made dependent upon the
same contingency.[6] For example, if property is given for life to the
first son of A to become a barrister with remainder to B absolutely,
the grant to the son is void unless either A is dead or a son of his
has already become a barrister by the time that the grant comes into
operation; there is no certainty that the identity of the first son to
become a barrister will be known within the life of A plus a further
period of 21 years. But the remainder to B is vested when the grant
comes into operation (his identity is known and no condition has
been attached to the grant of his interest) and it is valid. It will be
observed that the perpetuity rule is in no way concerned with the
question how long it may be before an interest vests in possession; it
is solely concerned with the question how long it may be before a
contingent interest vests (in the sense of ceasing to be contingent).

Had the grant been to the first son of A to become a barrister for
life, but if no son of A becomes a barrister then to B for life, with
remainders over, the remainder to B would have been void; it would
have been made dependent upon the same contingency which invalidated the grant to the first son of A to become a barrister.[7]

Powers of appointment

The owner of property may transfer it to trustees directing them
to hold it upon trust for such persons, or such members of a specified
class of persons, as D may appoint. D is then said to have a power
of appointment; he has the power to nominate the persons who are

---

[4] Rules of construction as to class gifts are discussed on pp. 151, 152, *post*.
[5] *Pearks* v. *Moseley* (1880) 5 App.Cas. 714.
[6] And not always then if the 1964 Act applies: see s. 6.
[7] See *Proctor* v. *Bishop of Bath and Wells* (1794) 2 Hy.Bl. 358.

to take the property. D is called the donee of the power. If D is at liberty to appoint the property to anyone he pleases, including himself, the power is said to be a general power of appointment, but if D may appoint the property only amongst members of a specified class of persons, such as his own children, the power is said to be a special power.[8]

For the purposes of the perpetuity rule the grant of a power of appointment is treated as the grant of an interest in property, so that the grant of the power is invalid unless when the grant comes into operation it is certain that the power will vest, if it vests at all, in an ascertainable person within the lives of persons who are living or conceived when the grant comes into operation plus a further period of 21 years. Moreover, with one exception, the grant of a power is also void if any appointment under it could be made after the end of the same period. For example, if property is settled on A (a bachelor) for life with remainder to A's first son for life, with remainder to such of that son's children as he by deed or will may appoint, the power given to A's son is void. The perpetuity period in this case is the life of A together with a further period of 21 years, and A's son might make an appointment which came into operation after the end of this period. This second rule, however, has no application to a general power of appointment granted to a single person which that person is at liberty to exercise at any time without obtaining the consent of any other person; and this is the exception referred to above.

Given the validity of the power, it is next necessary to consider the validity of any appointment which the donee of the power makes in the exercise of it. If the power is a general power, the appointment is treated in the same way as a gift of the appointor's own property. Any contingent interest created by the appointment will, therefore, be invalid if that interest might possibly vest after the end of the lives of persons who are living or conceived when the appointment comes into operation and a further period of 21 years. If the appointment is made under a special power of appointment a different rule obtains. Any contingent interest created by the appointment will be void if it might possibly vest after the end of the lives of any persons who were living or conceived when the deed or will which *created the power of appointment* came into operation together with a further period of 21 years. But in deciding whether there is any such possibility regard must be had to the facts as they were when the appointment came into operation. Two illustrations may make the distinction clearer.

---

[8] A power is also to be treated as a special power if exercisable only with the concurrence or consent of another person (1964 Act, s. 7, confirming the common law rule: see *Re Earl of Coventry's Indentures* [1974] Ch. 77.

(i) By the will of T property is settled upon trust for A (a bachelor) for life with remainder to such persons as A may by deed or will appoint. A exercises this power of appointment by his will, by which he appoints the property to all his children who attain the age of 25 equally. At his death, A has two children, *viz.* X, who is aged three, and Y, aged seven. The interest created by the appointment is contingent and will remain so until both X and Y attain the age of 25 (or the interest fails because they both die under that age). The gift is a class gift and it will remain contingent for both members of the class until the identity of every member of the class is known. (It must be noticed that the class consists of such of A's children *as attain the age of 25*.) The perpetuity period in this case is the lives of X and Y plus a further period of 21 years. The appointment has been made under a *general* power and (as stated above) the perpetuity period is the lives of persons who are living or conceived when the *appointment* comes into operation plus a further period of 21 years. The interest created by the appointment is, therefore, valid because there is, of course, no possibility that X or Y will attain the age of 25 after the end of his own life. It will be observed that in this case the age of 21 is not to be substituted for the age of 25 under the provisions of section 163 of the Law of Property Act 1925,[9] because that section applies only when the interest is bad as it stands, and in this case the interest created by the appointment is valid as it stands.

(ii) By the will of T property is settled on A (a bachelor) for life with remainder to such of his children as A by deed or will may appoint. A exercises this power of appointment by his will by which he appoints the property to all his children who attain the age of 25 equally. At A's death he has two children, *viz.* X, who is aged three, and Y, who is aged seven. In this case the perpetuity period is the life of A plus a further period of 21 years. As the appointment has been made under a *special* power of appointment, the perpetuity period consists of the lives of persons who were living or conceived when the instrument which *created the power of appointment* came into operation together with a further period of 21 years. Here again the interest created by the appointment is contingent, but in this case it is void as it stands. There is no certainty that we shall know the identities of the children of A who attain the age of 25 within 21 years from the death of A, bearing in mind that the younger son is aged three. However, if the appointment came into operation after 1925, *i.e.* if A died after that date, the appointment will be validated by section 163 of the Law of Property Act 1925, which will substitute the age of 21 for the offending age of 25. Had X been aged four instead of three at the death of A, the appointment would have been good as it stood and recourse would not have been had to the statute. It would then have been certain that the identities of the children of A who attained 25 would be known within 21 years of the death of A; it will be remembered that regard must be had to the facts existing when the *appointment* comes into operation in deciding whether there is any possibility that a contingent interest created by the appointment will vest after the end of the permitted period.

The Perpetuities and Accumulations Act 1964

This Act makes important changes in the rule against perpetuities. Its provisions are involved and difficult, and it is only possible to give a brief treatment of some of its provisions here. The Act (with minor exceptions) applies only to instruments taking effect after July 16, 1964, the date when the Act came into operation. Moreover, its main provisions are of a *relieving* character, *i.e.* they are designed to save an interest from invalidity if it *infringes* the perpetuity rule (as this rule stands apart from the Act); they have no application if the interest is valid without recourse to the Act. It is still necessary, therefore, to know the rule as it was before the Act. The following, in outline, are some of the main provisions of the Act:

(i) A settlor or testator may specify a period of years not exceeding 80 as the perpetuity period applicable to the disposition, instead of a life or lives in being and a further period of 21 years (section 1). (For an exception to this provision, see (vi) below.)

(ii) For the purposes of the perpetuity rule males under 14 and females under 12 and over 55 are presumed to be incapable of having children, but evidence is admissible to show that a living person will or will not be able to have a child (section 2). Previously no one was considered, for the purposes of the rule, to be too old to beget or bear children; the position with regard to the earliest possible age was uncertain. Thus a gift by will to the testator's brothers' and sisters' children who attained 21 might [10] infringe the rule if the testator's parents were alive when he died, by reason of the possibility of after-born brothers and sisters, even if both parents were over 60 at that time.

(iii) Perhaps the biggest change of all is that introduced by section 3, which, in effect, abolishes the principle that there is no " wait and see " in connection with the perpetuity rule. No interest is to be treated as void for breach of the rule until it becomes established that it *will* vest (if at all) after the end of the perpetuity period; but for this purpose " perpetuity period " is specially defined by reference to the lives of persons specified in the section.

---

[10] Sometimes the gift would be construed as referring only to the children living at the testator's death. See pp. 151, 152, *post*.

(iv) Section 163 of the Law of Property Act 1925 [11] is repealed and replaced by section 4 of the 1964 Act, which has broadly the same effect, but reduces the offending age in the instrument, not to 21, but to the nearest age that will avoid infringement of the perpetuity rule.

(v) Special relieving provisions in section 4 apply to class gifts; they have the effect of excluding those members of the class whose inclusion would render the gift void. There is also a special provision in section 5 which guards an interest from invalidity by reason of the possibility of a person's marrying one who is unborn when the instrument comes into operation; for example, apart from the Act, an interest conferred on the children of A (a bachelor) and any wife he may marry *who are living at the death of the survivor* of A and any such wife is void, as A may marry a woman not yet born and she may outlive him for more than 21 years.

(vi) Section 9 of the Act, on certain conditions, exempts from the perpetuity rule options given to a lessee to purchase the reversion, and provides that as regards options to acquire for valuable consideration any interest in land the perpetuity period (when applicable) shall be 21 years. Further, by section 10, when the perpetuity rule does apply, no contractual remedy is to be available after the end of the perpetuity period against the grantor of an interest created *inter vivos*: the significance of this provision will appear in a moment.

When the rule does not apply

The perpetuity rule has, or had, no application in the following cases (*inter alia*):

(i) *Contractual obligations*

Before the Act of 1964 the rule did not apply to an action, whether for damages or for specific performance, to enforce an obligation by which the defendant was contractually bound. For example, if a lease for 99 years conferred upon the tenant for the time being an option to purchase the reversion, and an action was brought against the original landlord upon his covenant to sell the reversion, the perpetuity rule had no application, since the landlord's obligation, though contingent (in the sense that the option when granted might or might not be exercised), was merely contractual.[12] It was otherwise if an action was brought against a subsequent owner of the reversion; the perpetuity rule then applied because the action was based, not on a contractual obligation, but on the ground that the grant of the option created an equitable interest [13] in the reversion which would be

---

[11] See p. 71, *ante*.
[12] *Hutton* v. *Watling* [1948] Ch. 26.
[13] In accordance with the principle that equity looks on that as done which ought to be done (see p. 12, *ante*).

enforceable by a decree of specific performance.[14] Similar principles
applied to any other option to purchase land: the original grantor (or
his estate) could always be sued, but the perpetuity rule applied to an
action against a successor in title of the grantor (other than his
personal representative). The Act of 1964 [15] has made important
changes in these rules which we have just considered, but it must be
remembered that the Act applies only to instruments taking effect
after its commencement.

(ii) *Leases and mortgages*

The perpetuity rule has no application to provisions in a lease, such
as a covenant for renewal, which are designed to regulate the relationship of landlord and tenant, and are not concerned with merely
collateral matters.[16] A similar exception applies to most provisions in
mortgages.

(iii) *Interests following a fee tail*

The perpetuity rule does not apply to a remainder which is to take
effect during the continuance of a fee tail or at the moment of its
determination. For example, if Blackacre is settled on A in tail with
a proviso that if at any time the tenant in tail of Blackacre should
become entitled to Whiteacre in fee simple, Blackacre is to go over
to B in tail, the remainder to B will be valid. This exception is
somewhat specious because the barring of the entail at any time would
defeat the remainder.

(iv) *Charities*

A gift over upon a certain event from one charity to another charity
is valid even if that event might occur after the end of the permitted
perpetuity period.

The Rule Against Perpetual Trusts

If property is settled upon trust to apply the income for some private
(*i.e.* non-charitable) purpose, the capital (or *corpus*) of the trust to be
held intact, the duration of the trust must be limited by the trust
instrument to a period which cannot exceed the lives of persons who
are living or conceived when the trust comes into operation, together
with a further period of 21 years.[17] (This at least appears to be the
purport of a rule which is not established with the same clarity as
the perpetuity rule proper.) Thus a gift of £5,000 upon trust to apply the

---

[14] *Woodall* v. *Clifton* [1905] 2 Ch. 257.
[15] ss. 9 and 10, *ante*.
[16] See Chap. 18.
[17] The 1964 Act does not affect the operation of this rule (see s. 15 (4)).

income in perpetuity for the maintenance of a tomb in a churchyard would be void under this rule. The rule is of little practical importance: it does not apply to charitable trusts, and on the other hand private trusts will generally be held void, regardless of any question of perpetuity, if the objects are not ascertainable human beneficiaries.

CHAPTER 15

THE ACCUMULATIONS RULE

THIS rule applies to directions to accumulate income. By such a direction is meant a direction (*e.g.* to trustees) that for a specified period the income from particular property is to be used to buy additional property, *e.g.* a direction that for a particular period the income from certain stocks or shares is to be used to buy further stocks or shares; the instrument may also direct that the income of the additional property is itself to be similarly applied. At common law such a direction was valid unless the period of the accumulation exceeded the period permitted by the modern perpetuity rule, but as the result of the case of *Thellusson* v. *Woodford* [1] Parliament thought it expedient to impose a much more stringent rule, and accordingly passed the Accumulations Act 1800. The rule today is to be found in the Law of Property Act 1925, ss. 164–166, as amended by the Perpetuities and Accumulations Act 1964 (for instruments taking effect after that Act). Today a direction to accumulate income if it is to be valid must be for one only of the following periods:

(i) The life of the grantor or settlor.

(ii) 21 years from the death of the grantor, settlor or testator.

(iii) The minority or respective minorities of any person or persons living or conceived at the death of the grantor, settlor or testator.

(iv) The minority or respective minorities of any person or persons who under the terms of the instrument directing accumulation would, for the time being, if of full age, be entitled to the income directed to be accumulated.

To these the Act of 1964 has added:

(v) 21 years from the date of the making of the disposition.

(vi) The minority or minorities of any person or persons living or conceived at that date.

In general a settlor (a term which for present purposes we shall use as including any grantor or testator) may choose whichever of the periods he prefers, but where the direction is that income shall be wholly or partially accumulated for the purchase of land only, the settlor must choose the fourth period if the direction is to be valid.

The rule has given rise to considerable difficulties of construction, and only a few points can be noticed here.

It will be observed that the only life period mentioned in the rule is

---

[1] (1805) 11 Ves. 112.

the life of the settlor. It follows that a *testator* cannot validly direct accumulation of income during the lifetime of any person.

The term " minority," which is used in the third, fourth and sixth periods, refers to the infancy of a given person, *i.e.* the period from the moment when that person is born until he attains full age. If the settlor decides to make use of the third or sixth period he must limit himself to the minorities of persons who are living or conceived at his death or the date of the settlement. But he may direct accumulation of income during the minorities of any such persons: those persons need not be beneficiaries. If the settlor decides to employ the fourth period he is not limited to the minorities of persons living or conceived at his own death or the date of the settlement, but on the other hand he can direct accumulation of income only during the minorities of certain beneficiaries, *i.e.* the beneficiaries who would for the time being if of full age be entitled to the income directed to be accumulated. For example, property may be settled on A (a bachelor) for life with remainder to such of A's children as are living at A's death, with a direction that if at A's death any such child is an infant the income from his share of the property shall be accumulated for him during his minority. This direction is valid under the fourth period, although it does not fall within the terms of the third or sixth periods as the direction is not to accumulate during the minorities of persons who are living or conceived at the death of the settlor or the date of the settlement.

It is provided by the Law of Property Act that the accumulations rule shall not extend to any provision:

(i) For payment of the debts of the settlor or any other person.

(ii) For raising portions for any issue of the settlor or of any beneficiary under the settlement or other instrument directing the accumulations.

(iii) Respecting the accumulation of the produce of timber or wood.

With the exception of a direction to accumulate income for the purpose of paying the debts of the settlor himself such a provision must comply with the perpetuity rule.

Breach of the rule

If a direction to accumulate income is for a period exceeding that permitted by the perpetuity rule, the direction is wholly void. If the direction does not infringe the perpetuity rule but does infringe the accumulations rule, the direction is not wholly void: it is good for whichever of the permitted periods is most appropriate to the particular case, and is void only for the excess over that period. This means that the court will select whichever of the permitted periods it considers to be most appropriate in the particular case, and the direction to accumulate will then take effect for this period or for the period directed in the instrument, whichever turns out to be the shorter. For example, if a testator directs that the income of certain property shall be accumulated during the life of A and that the property with its accumulations shall then be divided equally among all A's children living at his death, this direction does not infringe the perpetuity rule, but it does infringe the accumulations rule. In this case the court will select the period of 21 years from the death of the testator as being the most appropriate period. Accumulation of income will then take place during this 21 year period or the period of the life of A, whichever turns out to be the shorter. If A is still living at the end of the 21 year period accumulation of income must then cease, but distribution of the property cannot take place until the death of A: until A dies it cannot be ascertained who are the beneficiaries entitled to the property. The income accruing from the property between the end of the 21 year period and the death of A is to " go to and be received by the person or persons who would have been entitled thereto if such accumulation had not been directed "; this will usually be the person or persons entitled to the testator's residuary estate.

The rule in Saunders v. Vautier [2]

Under this rule if property is held on trust absolutely for a beneficiary who is of full age, the beneficiary can set aside any direction that the income of the property is to be accumulated for his benefit. He may in fact demand that the property itself be transferred to him by the trustees. For example, if a testator leaves property to A absolutely, but directs that the income of the property shall be accumulated for him until A reaches the age of 30, and A is of full age at the testator's death, A can put an end to the accumulation of the income at any time and require that the property itself be transferred to him. It would be otherwise if A's interest had been made *contingent* on his attaining 30. This rule is equally applicable when the beneficiary is a charity.

---

[2] (1841) 4 Beav. 115.

CHAPTER 16

EASEMENTS AND PROFITS

Easements

We now come to consider rights which a person may have against
the land of another, and the first of such rights that we shall consider
is the easement. An easement gives the right to use the land of another
in a particular way (a positive easement, *e.g.* a right of way) or the
right to prevent another from using his own land in a particular way
(a negative easement, *e.g.* a right of light, which prevents the neighbour from building on his land in such a way as unduly to obstruct
the flow of natural light to the windows of a house or other building).
An easement is a right *in rem*, which binds the land over which it
is exercisable in the hands of successive owners, and which can be
enforced by successive owners of the land for the benefit of which
it was granted.

The conditions of an easement

No right can be an easement unless it satisfies the following conditions:

(i) There must be a dominant tenement and a servient tenement,
i.e. one tenement to which the right is annexed and another tenement
which bears the burden of the right.

(ii) The right must accommodate the dominant tenement, *i.e.* in
some way add to its amenities.

(iii) The right must lie in grant, *i.e.* it must be capable of being
granted by deed.

(iv) The dominant and the servient tenements must be in different
hands, or more accurately the two tenements must not be both owned
and occupied by the same person in the same right.[1]

A right which does not satisfy these conditions will not be an
easement. It does not, however, necessarily follow that the law will
not recognise the right at all: it may be a perfectly valid right which
the law will recognise, *e.g.* as a licence, but it will not be an easement.

We may now consider a few points that arise on these four conditions. As an easement is a right against the land of another it is
obvious that there must be a servient tenement. The requirement
of a dominant tenement is not, however, obvious. It means that the

---

[1] *i.e.* the same capacity. Thus, if A owns one tenement beneficially and the
other as executor, the two tenements are not owned by A in the same right.

benefit of an easement must be annexed to a definite plot of land, so that only the occupiers of that plot have the benefit of the right. An easement cannot, therefore, be given to a grantee personally, *i.e.* independently of the ownership or occupation by him of land in the neighbourhood. In technical language an easement cannot exist in gross.

The requirement that the right must accommodate the dominant tenement is illustrated by *Hill* v. *Tupper*,[2] in which a canal company granted to a riparian owner the exclusive right to put pleasure boats on the canal. It was held that this right did not amount to an easement and that therefore the grantee of it could not himself maintain an action against another person who put out pleasure boats on the canal. No doubt the right accommodated the plaintiff's pocket, but it did not accommodate his tenement.

Because the right must lie in grant, *i.e.* be capable of being granted by deed, vague rights, such as rights of view or privacy, which cannot form the subject-matter of a grant, cannot be created as easements. A right for the inhabitants of neighbouring houses to use a pleasure ground for air and exercise has been held not too vague to exist as an easement,[3] however, and it seems now to be generally agreed that new *positive* easements can be created at the will of the parties, provided always that they comply with the four conditions set out above. But it may be that the category of *negative* easements is closed, and that except in relation to light, air and support (the only recognised negative easements) rights to restrict a neighbour in the use of his own land can be acquired only by means of appropriate restrictive covenants.[4]

Easements and natural rights

An easement is an acquired right, *i.e.* it must have been created by a grant of the right made by the owner of the servient tenement. A natural right is one that a landowner has as a necessary incident of his ownership of the land. Most natural rights are rights which a man has against his own land, *e.g.* the right to walk about it. There is, however, a natural right to support which gives to every landowner the right to have his land supported laterally by the land of his neighbour. If this support is withdrawn and in consequence the surface of his land subsides, he will have an action for damages against his neighbour. Any resulting damage to buildings can be recovered unless the weight of the building contributed to the subsidence, in which case *no* action will lie for breach of the natural right. Distinct from

---

[2] (1863) 2 H. & C. 121.
[3] *Re Ellenborough Park* [1956] Ch. 131, C.A.
[4] *Phipps* v. *Pears* [1965] 1 Q.B. 76, C.A. For restrictive covenants see p. 103, *post.*

the natural right of support is the easement of support, which, like every easement, requires acquisition by grant. An easement of support can be acquired which will give the right to have one's building supported by neighbouring land or a neighbouring building.

Acquisition of an easement

Apart from grant by Act of Parliament, an easement must have its origin in a grant of the right by deed or by will, but that grant may be express or implied or presumed. Presumed grant is otherwise known as prescription.

(1) *Express grant*

It is obvious that by arrangement between A and B, A, the fee simple owner of Blackacre, may grant B, the fee simple owner of Whiteacre, an easement against Blackacre. If the easement so granted is to be a legal easement, then (a) it must be granted for an interest equivalent to an estate in fee simple absolute in possession or a term of years absolute,[5] and (b) it must be granted by deed. Thus, an easement granted for the life of some person cannot be a legal easement although it can exist as an equitable easement. If an easement is granted otherwise than by deed, and if the grant is made for valuable consideration and there is either a sufficient written memorandum to satisfy section 40 of the Law of Property Act 1925, or there have been sufficient acts of part performance to dispense with the requirement of a written memorandum, the grant will create a valid equitable easement [6]; otherwise it will be void.

A legal easement is commonly created by reservation. For example if a landowner sells part of his land to another person he may reserve for the benefit of the land retained by him an easement (*e.g.* an easement of light) against the land sold. A mere reservation of an easement in a conveyance of land is capable of creating a legal easement after 1925.[7]

A conveyance of land may by express grant create an easement against land retained by the grantor although there are no words in the conveyance which purport to create such an easement. This strange result follows from the provisions of section 62 of the Law of Property Act 1925, which is known as the " general words " section because it imports into a conveyance of land words known to conveyancers as the " general words." By subsection (1) of this section, a conveyance of land shall be deemed to include and shall operate to convey with the land all " privileges, easements, rights and advantages whatsoever appertaining or reputed to appertain to the land, or any part thereof

---

[5] See Chap. 6.
[6] See Chaps. 5 and 11.
[7] Law of Property Act 1925, s. 65.

or, at the time of conveyance . . . enjoyed with, or reputed or known
as part or parcel of or appurtenant to the land or any part thereof."
For example, in *Wright* v. *Macadam* [8] a landlord allowed his tenant
to store his coal in a coal-shed belonging to the landlord although
the terms of the lease did not confer such a right upon the tenant.
When the lease expired the landlord granted a new lease to the tenant
which again made no mention of the right to store the coal in the
landlord's coal-shed. This new lease, however, was a " conveyance " [9]
within the terms of section 62, and the court held that the lease had
to be read as if it expressly conferred upon the tenant the right to
store his coal in the landlord's coal-shed. The privilege which during
the earlier lease was merely precarious and could be withdrawn by the
landlord at any time had now become an easement.

(2) *Implied grant*

(a) *In favour of the grantor of land.* If A grants part of his land
to B the law is reluctant to imply the grant of any easement against
the land granted to B in favour of that retained by A. A claim by A
to any such easement is an attempt by him to derogate (*i.e.* detract)
from his grant and it is a general principle of the law that a grantor
may not derogate from his grant.[10] In such a case the law is prepared
to imply the grant only of intended easements and of easements of
necessity. An intended easement is one which the court holds that the
parties in the circumstances must have intended to create. For example,
on the sale of a terrace house the court may be prepared to imply
the grant of an easement of support in favour of a neighbouring house
retained by the grantor. An easement of necessity is one which is
necessary for the continued occupation by the grantor of the land
retained by him. An easement of light will not be implied in favour
of the grantor of land, because a building is not unusable without the
benefit of natural light, but the grant of an easement of way against
the land granted will be implied in favour of the grantor if he would
have no other means of access to the land retained by him. The law
grants such an easement grudgingly, as it were, and it is a legal rule
that an easement of necessity can be used only to supply the needs
of the dominant tenement as they were at the date of the grant. For
example, if at the date of the grant the dominant tenement was used
for agricultural purposes, a right of way impliedly granted as an
easement of necessity cannot be used to cart building materials across

[8] [1949] 2 K.B. 744, C.A.
[9] This term includes any written instrument which is effective to pass a legal
estate in the land, *e.g.* a merely written lease for three years or less which is
effective at law, even though not under seal. (See p. 27, *ante*.)
[10] See p. 36, *ante*.

the servient tenement for some non-agricultural purpose.[11] On the
other hand the grantor of the land does have the right to select the
way to be enjoyed, provided that he acts reasonably.

(b) *In favour of the grantee of land.* When a landowner grants part
of his land to another person the law is much readier to imply the
grant of an easement against the land retained by the grantor for the
benefit of the land granted than it is to imply a grant in favour of the
grantor. There will be an implied grant of intended easements and
of easements of necessity and, under the doctrine of *Wheeldon* v.
Burrows,[12] there will be implied grant of all such continuous and
apparent rights as are capable of becoming easements, as are required
for the reasonable enjoyment of the land granted, and as were in fact
enjoyed for the benefit of that land immediately before the grant.[13]
For example, if there is a house upon the land granted which before
the grant enjoyed a flow of natural light across the land retained by
the grantor, there will be an implied grant of an easement of light
for the benefit of the house. The word " continuous " means " regularly
exercised," rather than strictly continuous. A right is " apparent "
for this purpose if its existence will be revealed by an inspection of
the land: a way, for example, is apparent if a visible track can be
seen.

The doctrine of *Wheeldon* v. *Burrows* is also applicable when a
landowner by contemporaneous grants disposes of parts of his land
to different persons, *e.g.* he makes devises thereof to different devisees
by his will. In such a case the grantee of what we may call the quasi-
dominant plot (*e.g.* the land with the house on it in the above example)
will get the *Wheeldon* v. *Burrows* easements against the quasi-servient
plot. The two plots will then be truly dominant and servient tenements.

There is a good deal of over-lap between the Law of Property Act
1925, s. 62, and the doctrine of *Wheeldon* v. *Burrows*, but there are
also distinctions between them. In particular, section 62 applies only
to a " conveyance " of land, *i.e.* an instrument effective to create a
legal estate in the land. *Wheeldon* v. *Burrows* is wider and applies
to a grant which creates only an equitable interest in the land, *e.g.* a
merely written lease for more than three years.[14] Again, *Wheeldon* v.
Burrows applies to rights that have been enjoyed *by* the common
owner of the quasi-dominant and quasi-servient plots, but it seems
that section 62 applies only to rights or privileges that have been
exercised *against* him, *e.g.* by his tenant.[15] On the other hand section

---

[11] *Corporation of London* v. *Riggs* (1880) 13 Ch.D. 798.
[12] (1879) 12 Ch.D. 31.
[13] Such rights are sometimes referred to as " quasi-easements."
[14] *Borman* v. *Griffith* [1930] 1 Ch. 493, and see p. 28, *ante*.
[15] See *Long* v. *Gowlett* [1923] 2 Ch. 177, *Ward* v. *Kirkland* [1967] Ch. 194.

62 is wider in that it applies to rights generally, not just to those that are " continuous and apparent." [16]

(3) Prescription

Long user may give rise to the presumed grant of an easement. For example, if the tenants of Blackacre have been in the habit of using a path across Whiteacre as a convenient means of access to Blackacre, and they have done this for a sufficiently long time, the law may presume that at some time in the past the fee simple owner of Whiteacre granted an easement of way across Whiteacre for the benefit of Blackacre. Prescription is based upon the acquiescence of the fee simple owners of the servient tenement in the open assertion of a right against that land by the tenants of the dominant tenement: the law infers the grant of an easement as the only possible explanation of this long-continued acquiescence. To justify this inference the user must have been as of right (*nec vi nec clam nec precario* [17]), and there must be evidence that the fee simple owners of the servient tenement have acquiesced in it; if, for example, the period of user was during a time when the servient tenement was let to a lessee the inference cannot normally be justified. [18]

We must now consider the different modes of prescription at common law and by statute.

(a) *At common law.* The common law had two modes of prescription. Under the earlier doctrine an easement is presumed if it appears that there has been user as of right since the beginning of legal memory (which by a fiction is fixed at A.D. 1189). Upon proof of user for a minimum period of 20 years the law presumes that there has been user since 1189, but this presumption is rebuttable and if it can be proved that user in fact began later than that date the claim will fail. In practice it is generally a matter of no great difficulty to prove that user began at a date later than 1189, *e.g.* when an easement of light is claimed, to prove that a building was first erected on that spot at some later date.

The common law has a great reverence for rights, or apparent rights, which have in fact been long enjoyed, and it therefore invented a second theory of prescription to supplement the first. This second mode of prescription at common law is known as the doctrine of the lost modern grant, whereas the earlier mode is known, somewhat inappropriately, as common law prescription—it would more aptly be called the doctrine of the lost ancient grant. To establish a claim

---

[16] It accordingly applies to profits, as well as to easements: *White* v. *Williams* [1922] 1 K.B. 727.

[17] Not by force nor secretly nor by permission.

[18] See p. 90, *post.* Conversely, user by a lessee of the dominant tenement generally enures for the benefit of the fee simple owner.

under the doctrine of the lost modern grant the claimant must show that there has been user as of right for a minimum period of 20 years. The court may then presume the grant of an easement in modern times which has since become lost. This mode of prescription has its own disadvantage, *viz.* that of uncertainty. One can say no more than that upon proof of at least 20 years' user the court may be prepared to infer a grant. Whether the court will do so depends upon all the circumstances of the particular case, and upon the likelihood or otherwise of a grant having been made.[19] Parliament, therefore, intervened with the Prescription Act 1832, which provides a third and alternative ground upon which a claim by prescription may be based.[20]

(b) *The Prescription Act 1832*

(i) *Easements other than light.* The Act provides that a claim to an easement other than light may be based upon proof of user for either 20 years or 40 years. In both cases the user must be as of right. Moreover, the user must be for 20 years of 40 years without interruption and next before (*i.e.* immediately preceding) some action in which the right to the easement is brought into question. It will be seen that user alone does not give rise to an easement under the provisions of the Act : the right is inchoate until some action is begun in which the claim to the easement is brought into question. The action may be brought by either side. Thus the dominant owner may issue a writ claiming a declaration that he has acquired an easement under the Act; or the right may be brought into question in an action brought by the servient owner, claiming an injunction to restrain the dominant owner from continuing to exercise the right, in answer to which the dominant owner claims that he has acquired an easement under the Act.

As we have seen, the user must be for 20 or 40 years without interruption immediately preceding the action, but the Act provides that no act shall rank as an interruption unless the dominant owner has acquiesced in it for a full year [21] after becoming aware of it and of the person responsible for it. For this reason it is often stated that user for 19 years and one day is as good as user for 20 years. This

[19] It seems, however, that a claim cannot be defeated by proof that no such grant has in fact been made (*Dalton* v. *Angus* (1881) 6 App.Cas. 740, *Tehidy Minerals Ltd.* v. *Norman* [1971] 2 Q.B. 528, C.A.).

[20] It is normal practice to plead all three modes of prescription. A claim might fail under the Act yet succeed on the basis of lost modern grant. (See *Hulbert* v. *Dale* [1909] 2 Ch. 570; *Pugh* v. *Savage* [1970] 2 Q.B. 373, C.A.)

[21] If the dominant owner has made strong protests to the servient owner against interference with the exercise of the right, failure for a year to make further protests will not necessarily amount to acquiescence during that period : see *Davies* v. *Du Paver* [1953] 1 Q.B. 184, C.A.

statement is a half-truth. It is not possible after user for merely 19 years and a day to issue a writ claiming an easement, because it will not then be possible to prove user for the requisite period of 20 years. What is meant by the statement is that, if the claimant submits to the interruption for 364 days and then immediately issues his writ, he will be able to establish user for 20 years for the purposes of the Act. The interruption, having lasted for less than a full year, will not rank as an interruption for the purposes of the claim.

On these matters then the rules are the same whether the claim is based upon the shorter or the longer period of user. But obviously there are differences. Not all these differences are clearly established by decisions on the Act, but the following points must be noticed.

Disabilities. If the claim is based upon the shorter period of user, section 7 of the Act requires that there shall be deducted from the period of user any periods during which the servient owner has been an infant, lunatic, or tenant for life. The claim will not succeed unless there still remains a period of 20 years after these deductions have been made. If the claim is based upon the longer period of user no deduction is to be made under section 7, but section 8 of the Act provides that if the claim is to a right of " way or other convenient watercourse or use of water " there shall be deducted from the period of user any periods when the servient tenement has been held under a tenancy for life or a lease for a term exceeding three years, provided that the claim to the easement is resisted by a reversioner within three years after the end of the tenancy for life or lease. Obviously something has gone wrong with the wording of the Act, because a right of way is not a watercourse, whether convenient or inconvenient. It is therefore doubtful whether section 8 applies to all easements other than light, or only to rights of way and water. Even when the section applies, deduction is not to be made unless the claim to the easement is resisted by a reversioner within three years after the determination of the tenancy for life or lease. Moreover the word " reversioner " [22] has been strictly construed and, it has been held, does not include a remainderman.[23] Thus, if Whiteacre is settled on A for life with remainder to B in fee simple and the tenant of an adjoining property, Blackacre, uses a way across Whiteacre for upwards of 40 years, there can be no deduction of A's tenancy for life. B is a remainderman, not a reversioner. But if during the period of user Whiteacre had been held under a lease for more than three years, the period of the lease would have had to be deducted from the period of user, provided that the landlord of Whiteacre had resisted

---

[22] More accurately " person entitled to any reversion."
[23] *Symons* v. *Leaker* (1885) 15 Q.B.D. 629.

the claim to the easement within three years after the end of the lease. The landlord is a reversioner.

Consents. If permission for the exercise of the right has been sought from the servient owners from time to time the claim to an easement will generally fail. The user is not in such a case " as of right," as the Act requires. There is, however, one exception to this rule. If user for the longer period is established, a merely oral consent given *before* the user began will not defeat the claim. This is because the Act provides that a claim based on the longer period of user shall be indefeasible unless the right has been enjoyed by written consent or agreement, and some meaning must be given to the reference to written consent. This, at least, appears to be the position resulting from some ill-drafted and seemingly contradictory provisions of the Act.

Strange as it may seem, it sometimes pays to base a claim upon the shorter period of user, even if the longer period can be proved, because there is no provision for deduction of leases when the claim is based upon the shorter period, as there is when it is based upon the longer period. If, however, the servient tenement was let when the user began, then, even if the claim is based on the shorter period, the period of the lease will generally have to be deducted upon the general principle that prescription is founded upon the acquiescence of the fee simple owner of the servient tenement: the fee simple owner was not then in a position to prevent the user. (The position is quite different if the lease was granted *after* the user began: the servient owner has then, by his own act, put it out of his power to prevent further user.) [24]

(ii) *The easement of light.* The Act provides that a claim to an easement of light may be founded upon proof of actual enjoyment of the light for a period of 20 years without interruption and next before some action in which the right is brought into question. Proof that the user was by virtue of written consent given by the servient owner will defeat the claim, but in other respects the user need not have been as of right, nor need it have been by or on behalf of one fee simple owner against another: actual user suffices. In consequence a lessee can acquire an easement of light under the Act against land which is occupied by another tenant of his own landlord or which is occupied by the landlord himself: this is possible only in the case of the easement of light and only when the claim is brought under the Act of 1832. No provision is made for deduction of periods of disability of the servient owner. [25]

---

[24] *Palk* v. *Shinner* (1852) 18 Q.B. 215; *Pugh* v. *Savage* [1970] 2 Q.B. 373.
[25] A further distinction between the provisions of the Act with regard to the easement of light and those relating to other easements is that only the latter bind the Crown.

To enable a landowner to prevent his neighbour from acquiring an easement of light without the necessity of erecting a screen to obstruct the flow of light to his neighbour's building, the Rights of Light Act 1959 provides for the registration as a local land charge [26] of a light obstruction notice, specifying the size and position of a notional obstruction. The dominant owner may then sue for a declaration that he has acquired an easement of light as if there had been an actual obstruction, and the Act provides that in such an action the claimant may treat his user as having begun a year earlier than in fact it did.

Kinds of easements

The commonest easements are those of way and of light.

An easement of way is often restricted, *e.g.* to the use of foot passengers. The extent of the easement depends upon the terms of the grant, express or implied,[27] or upon the nature and extent of user in the case of an easement acquired by prescription.[28] The maintenance and repair of the way are generally the responsibility of the grantee of the easement.

An easement of light gives the right, according to the ordinary notions of mankind, to sufficient light for the use of the premises as a dwelling-house or for ordinary business purposes.[29] A right to a greater amount of light than this cannot be acquired as an easement. It will be observed, therefore, that an obstruction of the flow of light which substantially diminishes the amount of light reaching the windows of a building will not necessarily constitute an infringement of an easement of light which is enjoyed for the benefit of that building. The question is not how much light has been taken away, but how much light is left; if this is sufficient for ordinary dwelling or business purposes no action will lie.

Other common easements are those of support and of water (*e.g.* a right to water cattle at another's stream) and the easement of eaves-drop, which gives the right to allow rainwater to discharge itself from the roof of one's building on to a neighbour's land.

Profits

A profit is similar to an easement in that it also is a right against the land of another, but whereas an easement is said to be a right without profit a profit gives the right to take something from another's land which is either part of the soil itself (*e.g.* a right to take gravel)

---

[26] Such a register is kept by certain local authorities: see Chap. 22.
[27] See, *e.g. Corporation of London* v. *Riggs*, p. 86, *ante.*
[28] See *British Railways Board* v. *Glass* [1965] Ch. 538, C.A.
[29] *Colls* v. *Home and Colonial Stores Ltd.* [1915] A.C. 599.

or part of the produce of the soil (*e.g.* a right to pasture one's cattle on a neighbour's land or to take fish from his stream). But a right to take water from another's stream is an easement, not a profit, because the water is not regarded as being part of the soil or of its produce.

A profit may be a several profit or a profit in common (or a common). A several profit gives to the owner of it the right to take the subject-matter, *e.g.* the fish, from another's land to the exclusion of everyone else, including the servient owner himself. A profit in common gives the right to take the subject-matter in common with others. It depends upon the terms of the grant whether a profit is a several profit or a profit in common, but several profits are comparatively rare: hence the term " common " is often used as a synonym for profit.[30]

Profits may also be divided into profits appurtenant and profits in gross. A profit appurtenant is one the benefit of which is annexed by the grant to a dominant tenement. It, therefore, resembles an easement, and indeed a profit appurtenant must conform to the four conditions of an easement.[31] Hence it is a contradiction in terms to claim as a profit appurtenant a right to fish in another's stream for commercial purposes: such a right does not accommodate the dominant tenement.[32] A profit in gross is one which is given to the grantee personally, *i.e.* irrespective of his ownership or occupation of land: there is no dominant tenement.

Mention may also be made of the profit *pur cause de vicinage*; this is a right which commoners of adjoining commons[33] may have to allow their cattle to stray on to the neighbouring common.

Modes of acquisition

The modes of acquiring a profit are similar to the modes of acquiring an easement, and it will be simplest to notice the main differences:

(i) The doctrine of *Wheeldon* v. *Burrows* does not apply to profits. This difference, however, is not of great importance, because section 62 of the Law of Property Act 1925 does apply to profits and, as we have seen, the doctrine of *Wheeldon* v. *Burrows* is largely superseded by the statutory provision.[34]

(ii) A profit in gross cannot be claimed by prescription under the Act of 1832, although it can be claimed under the other modes of prescription.

---

[30] Rights of common are now registrable with the appropriate local authority under the Commons Registration Act 1965, and existing rights, not registered before July 31, 1970, thereupon ceased to be exercisable.

[31] See p. 82, *ante*.

[32] *Harris* v. *Earl of Chesterfield* [1911] A.C. 623.

[33] *i.e.* (in this sense) land subject to a right of common.

[34] See p. 86, *ante*.

(iii) If a profit is claimed under the Act of 1832 the periods of user provided by the Act are 30 years and 60 years, instead of the periods of 20 years and 40 years provided for easements. In the main there are the same differences as for easements between claims founded on the shorter and those founded on the longer period. For example, if the claim is founded on the shorter period a deduction will have to be made for any periods when the servient owner has been under one of the disabilities mentioned in section 7 of the Act. But section 8 of the Act, which applies to a claim to an easement based on the longer period of user, has no application when a profit is claimed on the ground of user for 60 years. There is, therefore, no provision for deduction of periods of leases of the servient tenement; but such leases have to be taken into account in deciding whether there has been that acquiescence in the user by the fee simple owners of the servient tenement which is essential to prescription (except when an easement of light is claimed under the Act), and this is so whether the claim to a profit is based on the shorter or the longer period of user.[35] In the case of commons, deductions must also be made of periods of non-user for reasons of animal health or government requisition; but such non-user is not an interruption for the purposes of the 1832 Act.[36]

Kinds of profits

The most important profit is the profit of pasture, which gives the right to pasture cattle on another's land. The number of cattle must be limited in some way, if only by the ability of the servient tenement to support the cattle.[37] Mention has already been made of the profit of piscary (*i.e.* the right to fish in another's stream) and the profit in the soil (*i.e.* the right to take part of the soil itself, such as sand), and there are other possible profits.

Extinguishment of Easements and Profits

The owner of an easement or profit may release his hereditament,[38] and this release may be express or implied. Implied release requires evidence of an intention to abandon the right. Non-user of itself does not necessarily show such an intention: thus release of an easement of way cannot be inferred from non-user during a period when the owner of the easement of way temporarily enjoyed a more convenient means of access to his property. Again, if a house enjoys the benefit

---

[35] *Davies* v. *Du Paver* [1953] 1 Q.B. 184, C.A.
[36] Commons Registration Act 1965, s. 16.
[37] A right of common registered under the 1965 Act is limited to the number of cattle for which it is registered.
[38] Easements, profits and rentcharges are known as incorporeal hereditaments; they are rights in land which do not give possession of the land itself but are capable of being inherited.

of an easement of light, knocking down the house will not show an
intention to abandon the easement if the owner intends to re-build
the house and the house when re-built has windows which enjoy
substantially the same light. The question is always whether an
intention to abandon can properly be inferred from all the circumstances of the particular case.

An easement or profit will also become extinguished if the same
person becomes both owner and possessor of the dominant and the
servient tenements, provided that he holds the two tenements in the
same capacity.

Approvement and enclosure are means by which the waste land of
a manor may become freed from the rights of the commoners. Both
procedures are subject to complicated statutory enactments and require
ministerial and parliamentary approval, respectively.

Public Rights of Way

Apart from creation by special statutory provision, a public right of
way must have its origin in a dedication of the way to the public by
the land-owner or land-owners concerned, coupled with an acceptance
of the way by the public. Dedication may be express or it may be
presumed from user of the way by the public as of right to the
knowledge of the land-owner or land-owners concerned. Dedication
may be presumed at common law, in which case no particular period
of user is prescribed by the law, or it may be presumed under the
Highways Act 1959. Under the Act dedication is to be presumed upon
proof of uninterrupted user as of right for 20 years next before the
right of user is brought into question unless there is sufficient evidence
that there was no intention during the period of user to dedicate a
way to the public. Absence of intention to dedicate may be proved
in a number of ways provided by the Act, *e.g.* by exhibiting a suitable
notice, or it may be proved in any other way, *e.g.* by the land-owner's
closing the way to the public for one day in each year (a method
commonly adopted).

It will be observed that under the Act the relevant period of user
is that of 20 years next before the right of user is brought into question.
The right can be brought into question in any way, *e.g.* by the landowner's turning back the public. It is not necessary that an action
should be brought on either side (as is necessary for the establishment
of an easement under the Prescription Act 1832).

Claims by Fluctuating Bodies of Persons

(a) Quasi-easements

A fluctuating body of persons (other than the public at large) may claim a right in the nature of an easement. For example, the inhabitants of a particular village may claim the right to pass across private land in order to reach the parish church (a right known as a church-way). Such a right cannot subsist as a true easement, because, as we have seen,[39] an easement must have its origin in a grant, and a grant cannot be made to such a fluctuating body of persons. A valid foundation for the right may, however, be established under the doctrine of custom. The main requisites of a valid custom are that the right claimed should be limited to a defined locality known to the law, such as a parish or manor, and that the right should have been claimed continuously since 1189. Proof of user for 20 years raises a rebuttable presumption that the right has been claimed continuously since 1189. (Compare the similar rule with regard to common law prescription.[40])

(b) Quasi-profits

A fluctuating body of persons cannot directly claim a profit, because a profit, like an easement, must have its origin in a grant. Nor is such a body allowed to claim a right in the nature of a profit under the doctrine of custom.[41] But there are two very restricted methods by which the claim may be established. First, if the right has been granted by the Crown, the Crown may have incorporated the fluctuating body of persons,[42] in which case as a corporation it becomes a competent grantee. Moreover, when the right has been granted by the Crown incorporation may sometimes be presumed. Secondly, if it can be established that from time immemorial the right has been claimed by a local corporation, as well as by the fluctuating body of persons, the court may presume the grant of a profit to the corporation upon trust for itself and the fluctuating body.[43]

Licences

Permission to use another person's land which does not fall into any other category (*e.g.* is not an easement or a profit or a lease) is known as a licence. Normally at any rate, a licence does not create an interest in the land, although it does give certain rights to the licensee.

It follows that a licence, unlike an easement or a lease, is enforceable only between the parties (*in personam*), not against the land itself (*in rem*).[44] Licences generally are of three kinds:

---

[39] See p. 82, *ante.*
[40] See p. 87, *ante.*
[41] *Alfred F. Beckett Ltd.* v. *Lyons* [1967] Ch. 449, C.A.
[42] The Crown has power to confer the status of corporation upon any body of persons.
[43] *Goodman* v. *Mayor of Saltash* (1882) 7 App.Cas. 633.
[44] *King* v. *David Allen & Sons, Billposting, Ltd.* [1916] 2 A.C. 54; *Clore* v. *Theatrical Properties Ltd.* [1936] 3 All E.R. 483.

(i) *Bare licence*

A bare licence is a licence granted gratuitously which is not coupled with the grant of an interest in the land, *e.g.* the licence which one necessarily grants to one's guests. Such a licence may be revoked at any time.

(ii) *Licence coupled with an interest*

A licence may be coupled with the grant of an interest in the land, as when standing timber is sold on terms that the purchaser is to sever the timber: the sale of the timber on these terms implies the grant to the purchaser of a licence to enter the land in order to obtain the timber. Such a licence is irrevocable so long as the interest to which it is annexed lasts, and unless otherwise agreed it can be assigned.

(iii) *Licence for value*

This is a licence granted for value but not coupled with the grant of any interest in the land, *e.g.* the licence to enter and view the performance which is implied on the sale of a theatre or cinema ticket. At common law such a licence was revocable at any time,[45] but now as the result of the intervention of equity it is irrevocable for so long as the parties must have intended it to be so. For example, unless otherwise agreed the licence implied on the sale of a theatre or cinema ticket is irrevocable for the duration of the performance (provided of course that the purchaser does not misbehave himself in the theatre).[46]

Although, as mentioned above, a licence does not normally create an interest in land such as can be enforced against a person acquiring the land from the licensor, it seems that a licence may arise in such circumstances that in equity not only the licensor himself but also persons claiming through him may be estopped from revoking it. If the licensee has incurred expense or some other detriment in relation to the land, *e.g.* by building on it,[47] on the faith of an express or implied promise not to revoke the licence, it may be regarded as being coupled with an equitable interest in the land, and enforceable against any person acquiring the land except a bona fide purchaser for value without notice.[48]

---

[45] *Wood* v. *Leadbitter* (1845) 13 M. & W. 838.

[46] *Hurst* v. *Picture Theatres Ltd.* [1915] 1 K.B. 1, C.A. See generally *Winter Garden Theatre (London) Ltd.* v. *Millennium Productions Ltd.* [1948] A.C. 173; *Hounslow L.B.C.* v. *Twickenham Garden Developments Ltd.* [1971] Ch. 233.

[47] *Dillwyn* v. *Llewelyn* (1862) 4 De G.F. & J. 517; *Inwards* v. *Baker* [1965] 2 Q.B. 29.

[48] See *Errington* v. *Errington and Woods* [1952] 1 K.B. 290; *E. R. Ives Investment Ltd.* v. *High* [1967] 2 Q.B. 379, in both of which the licence was, in effect, contractual. The scope of the principle of equitable, or proprietary, estoppel is the subject of much controversy.

It should be noted that the right (or licence) of a deserted spouse to remain in the matrimonial home has been held not to be capable of binding third parties.[49] Such a right is now governed by the Matrimonial Homes Act 1967,[50] under which a spouse who is not the owner or part-owner of the matrimonial home has certain " rights of occupation," which are a charge on the other spouse's estate or interest and registrable as such under the Land Charges Act 1972.

---

[49] *National Provincial Bank Ltd.* v. *Ainsworth* [1965] A.C. 1175.
[50] As amended by the Matrimonial Proceedings and Property Act 1970.

CHAPTER 17

RENTCHARGES

A RENTCHARGE is a rent charged upon land, not being a rent payable to a landlord under a lease (a rent payable to a landlord is known as a rent service). To be a legal rentcharge the rent must be created by deed and must be either perpetual or for a term of years absolute and must be in possession.[1]

Rentcharges are still created today in some parts of the country upon a sale of land, *i.e.* the purchaser, instead of paying a lump sum, covenants to pay an annual sum of money for a fixed term of years or in perpetuity and the obligation to pay this sum is charged upon the land.

Since 1925 a rentcharge may be charged directly upon land or it may be charged upon another rentcharge.

Remedies for recovery

The owner of a rentcharge which is charged directly upon land has the following remedies for the recovery of the rent if it is not paid.

(i) *Action on the covenant*

The original covenantee, if still the owner of the rentcharge, may sue the original covenantor upon his covenant to pay in the deed creating the rentcharge. Such an action against the original covenantor may also be brought by an assignee of the rentcharge if the benefit of the covenant was expressly assigned to him. But the benefit of the covenant does not pass upon an assignment of the rentcharge without an express assignment of the benefit of the covenant.[2]

(ii) *Action against terre tenant*

At common law the freehold tenant in possession of the land (the *terre tenant*) is personally liable for the rent to the owner of the rentcharge for the time being, and this is so even if the amount of the rent exceeds the current annual value of the land. Moreover, if the land has been split up, the *terre tenant* of any part of the land is liable for the whole of the rentcharge, unless the owner of the rent has agreed to its being apportioned.

(iii) *Statutory remedies*

By the Law of Property Act 1925, s. 121, the owner of a rent-

---

[1] See p. 16, *ante.*
[2] *Grant* v. *Edmondson* [1931] 1 Ch. 1.

charge is given three statutory remedies for its recovery. First, if the rent or any part of it is 21 days in arrears, the owner of the rent-charge can distrain for it. Secondly, if the rent or any part of it is 40 days in arrears, he may enter and take possession of the land and take the rents and profits until he has raised all the arrears. Thirdly, if the rent or any part of it is 40 days in arrears, the owner of the rentcharge may grant a lease of the land to a trustee upon trust to raise the arrears by mortgaging the leasehold term or any other reasonable means.

(iv) *Re-entry*

If the instrument creating the rentcharge so provides, but not other-wise, the owner of a rentcharge which has fallen into arrears may re-enter upon the land and claim the fee simple (or other estate of the grantor of the rentcharge).

The Law of Property Act 1925, s. 122, provides that when a rentcharge is charged upon another rentcharge, the owner of the subrentcharge may appoint a receiver of the main rent if the subrent-charge or any part of it falls 21 days into arrears. The receiver will then obtain payment of the main rent and out of it pay to the owner of the sub-rent what is due to him.

Discharge

The Law of Property Act 1925, s. 191, contains provisions whereby a landowner may obtain the discharge of a rentcharge to which his land is subject upon payment to the owner of the rentcharge of a lump sum representing the capital value, determined in accordance with the section.

CHAPTER 18

COVENANTS CONCERNING LAND

(A) Covenants in leases

1. BETWEEN the original landlord and the original tenant there is
privity of contract, *i.e.* the parties have bound themselves personally
to one another upon any covenants into which they have entered in
the lease. This contractual liability subsists throughout the whole term
of the lease,[1] notwithstanding the death of either party, *i.e.* his personal representatives remain liable on his covenants in the lease.[2]
Again, the original landlord is liable to the original tenant upon the
landlord's covenants in the lease even if in the meantime the landlord has assigned the reversion to another person. Similarly the
original tenant is liable to the original landlord upon the tenant's
covenants in the lease, even if in the meantime the original tenant has
assigned the lease to another person. Upon an assignment of the
reversion the benefit of the tenant's covenants can be expressly assigned
to the assignee of the reversion, and he can then sue the original
tenant upon the tenant's covenants in the lease. Similary upon an
assignment of the lease the benefit of the landlord's covenants can
be expressly assigned to the assignee of the lease, and he can then
sue the original landlord upon the landlord's covenants.

2. The relationship of landlord and tenant subsists between the
owner of the reversion *for the time being* and the owner of the lease
for the time being, and there is said to be privity of estate between
them. When privity of estate subsists the landlord for the time being
is liable to the tenant for the time being on such of the landlord's
covenants in the lease as touch and concern the land, and similarly
the tenant is liable to the landlord on such of the tenant's covenants
as touch and concern the land.[3] A covenant touches and concerns
the land in this sense if it regulates the position of the landlord and
the tenant in those capacities. All covenants that are commonly
found in leases do touch and concern the land, *e.g.* a landlord's

---

[1] It is otherwise with the *implied* obligations of landlord and tenant (see
Chap. 10); the landlord or tenant is liable only for breaches committed while
he held the reversion or the lease, respectively.

[2] To the extent of the deceased's assets. The same rule applies to a periodical
tenancy: the estate of the deceased tenant remains liable for the rent until the
tenancy is validly determined by notice (*Youngmin* v. *Heath* [1974] 1 W.L.R.
135, C.A.).

[3] The rule in *Spencer's Case* (1583) 5 Co.Rep. 16 (applying where the lease
has been assigned); Law of Property Act 1925, ss. 141–142 (applying where the
reversion has been assigned).

covenant for quiet enjoyment, or to maintain the exterior of the premises in repair, or a tenant's covenant to pay the rent, to pay tenant's rates and taxes, to maintain the premises in repair, or not to use the premises otherwise than for the purposes of a private dwelling-house. An example of a covenant that does not concern and touch the land is a landlord's covenant to sell the reversion to the tenant: such a covenant does not regulate the relationship of landlord and tenant, but contemplates its determination by the exercise by the tenant of his option to purchase the landlord's interest.[4]

There is an important distinction between liability by privity of contract and liability by privity of estate. As we have seen, each of the original parties remains liable by privity of contract upon his covenants *throughout the term of the lease*, but a landlord or tenant who is liable only by privity of estate is liable only for breaches of covenant committed by him while he held the reversion or the lease, as the case may be. An example may make the position clearer. Suppose that L is the original landlord and T the original tenant, and suppose that T has assigned the lease to A and that A in his turn has assigned the lease to B. Suppose further that the lease contains a tenant's repairing covenant and that B breaks this covenant. L may sue T, who cannot excuse himself by the plea that he had assigned the lease before the breach of covenant occurred. T is liable by privity of contract and remains liable for breach of tenant's covenants committed at any time during the lease. Alternatively, L may sue B, the tenant who in fact committed the breach of covenant: B is liable by privity of estate. But L cannot sue A: A was liable only by privity of estate and ceased to be liable, as to future breaches of tenant's covenants, when he parted with the lease. It may be noticed that an assignee of the reversion who obtains the benefit of a tenant's covenant may sue the tenant for a breach of covenant committed before the assignment of the reversion.[5]

3. If the landlord sues the original tenant for breach of a tenant's covenant committed after the original tenant had parted with the lease, the original tenant may claim indemnity from the assignee of the lease who in fact committed the breach. Thus, in the above illustration, if L sued T in respect of the breach committed by B, T could claim indemnity from B. This is a common law right. It will be observed that T could not claim indemnity from A under this common law right; the common law right of indemnity is potentially defective, therefore, in that B may prove not to be worth suing. Hence, it became the practice of conveyancers to insert into an assignment of a

[4] The option is enforceable on the basis discussed at p 76, *ante.*
[5] Law of Property Act 1925, s. 141; *Re King* [1963] Ch. 459, C.A.; *London and County (A. & D.) Ltd.* v. *Wilfred Sportsman Ltd.* [1971] Ch. 764, C.A.

lease an express covenant by the assignee to indemnify the assignor against liability for any breach of a tenant's covenant committed after the assignment, whether by the assignee himself or by a later assignee. Such an indemnity covenant is now implied by the Law of Property Act 1925, s. 77, in an assignment for value. Thus, in our last illustration, if L sued T and such an indemnity covenant, express or implied, was included in the assignment of the lease by T to A, T could claim indemnity from A in respect of the breach committed by B. If A then proves not to be worth suing, T has only himself to blame for assigning to an insubstantial assignee. For this reason upon an assignment of a lease care should be taken to ensure that the assignee will be worth suing should occasion arise.

It may be noticed that upon an assignment of the reversion there is no statutory provision implying an indemnity covenant. An express covenant of indemnity should, therefore, be included in the conveyance.

(B) Covenants not in Leases

Covenants not in leases are commonly known as " vendor and purchaser covenants " because commonly entered into upon the sale by a vendor of part of his land: the purchaser may then enter into covenants with the vendor (*e.g.* a covenant to use the land bought for the purposes only of a private dwelling-house) which are intended to bind the land purchased for the benefit of the land retained by the vendor, and vice versa. The principal rules are then as follows.

1. As between the original covenantor and the original covenantee there is privity of contract: in this respect the rules are similar to those governing covenants in leases. Thus, unless the covenant is specially worded the original covenantee can sue the original covenantor for damages for a breach of the covenant even if in the meantime the covenantor has parted with the land affected. Moreover, in general, the benefit of the covenant can be expressly assigned and the assignee will then have the same right of action against the original covenantor as the original covenantee would have had.

2. If the covenant is taken for the benefit of land owned by the covenantee, the *benefit* of the covenant may pass without express assignment on a transfer of that land. Originally the covenantee had to have a legal estate in the land and the transferee of that land had to possess the same legal estate. For covenants made after 1925 this rule has been somewhat relaxed by section 78 of the Law of Property Act 1925, which enables persons claiming under the original covenantee to enforce the covenant even if they are not possessed of the same legal estate. For example, if the covenant is made after 1925 between adjoining fee simple owners, a lessee of the covenantee's land can enforce the covenant.

At common law the *burden* of the covenant did not pass with the land of the covenantor, even though the covenant was clearly intended to regulate the use of the land. Thus, although at common law a transferee of the covenantee's land might be able to enforce the covenant against the original covenantor, neither the original covenantee nor a transferee of his land could enforce the covenant against a subsequent owner of the covenantor's land: the covenant could be enforced only against the original covenantor (and his estate after his death). There is, in effect, a limited exception to this rule derived from the principle that one who claims the benefit of a grant must accept its burdens. For example, it was decided in *Halsall* v. *Brizell* [6] that, if a purchaser is given the right to use roads which pass across another's land subject to the obligation to contribute to the cost of maintaining the roads, he may not use the roads without making the contribution, and a subsequent owner of the purchaser's land is in the same position.

For the purposes of the above rules it is immaterial whether a covenant is positive or negative.

3. Very much more liberal rules were established by equity with regard to *restrictive* covenants. The test for determining whether the covenant is positive or negative is the substance, and not the form, of the covenant, *i.e.* the test is whether or not the performance of the covenant involves the expenditure of labour or money. Thus, a covenant to use premises for the purposes only of a private dwelling-house is a restrictive, or negative, covenant, but a covenant not to allow a building to fall into disrepair is a positive covenant for this purpose.

If a restrictive covenant affecting the covenantor's land is taken for the benefit of land belonging to the covenantee, equity, on certain conditions, is prepared to treat the covenant as creating an interest in the covenantor's land similar to a negative easement. The covenantee's land may then be regarded as in the nature of a dominant tenement and that of the covenantor as in the nature of a servient tenement. The analogy must not be pressed too far, but—and this is the important point—it follows that the burden of the covenant will pass on a transfer of the covenantor's land, so that a subsequent owner of that land will be bound by the covenant as if it had been a negative easement. This equitable principle is known as the doctrine of *Tulk* v. *Moxhay*. [7]

As the interest in the covenantor's land which was created by this doctrine was equitable, it followed that the covenant could not be

---

[6] [1957] Ch. 169. Se also *E. R. Ives Investment Ltd.* v. *High* [1967] 2 Q.B. 379, C.A.
[7] (1848) 2 Ph. 774.

enforced against a subsequent purchaser for value of the legal estate in the covenantor's land who acquired the land without notice, actual or constructive, of the covenant. This rule still applies to covenants created before 1926, but a restrictive covenant created after 1925 (and not being in a lease) is registrable as a land charge under the Land Charges Act 1972.[8] In accordance with the usual rule, registration of the interest will constitute actual notice of its existence to anyone who afterwards acquires the covenantor's land, and failure to register the interest will render it void against a subsequent purchaser of that land (even if he has actual notice of the interest).

The conditions which must be satisfied before the doctrine of *Tulk* v. *Moxhay* will come into operation are of a complicated character and only some of the more important rules can be considered here.

(a) The plaintiff must own some interest in the land for the benefit of which the covenant was taken. Thus even the original covenantee cannot rely upon the equitable doctrine once he has parted with his land.

(b) If the plaintiff is not the original covenantee, but a subsequent owner of the land, he must prove that the benefit of the covenant has passed to him. This he may do in one of three ways:

(i) *Assignment*

He may show that the benefit of the covenant was assigned to him, expressly or by necessary implication,[9] at the time when he acquired the dominant land.

(ii) *Annexation*

If the wording of the covenant made it plain that the benefit was intended to be taken, not only by the original covenantee, but also by subsequent owners of the land, the benefit will have passed to the plaintiff without express assignment. Where the plaintiff holds part only of the original covenantee's land, it may be difficult to establish that the benefit is attached to one part, rather than to the land as a whole.[10]

(iii) *Building scheme*

When land is developed, *e.g.* by the construction of a housing estate, the developer may require each purchaser of a plot to enter into restrictive covenants designed to maintain the general character of the estate and the value of the property. On certain conditions these covenants then operate as a kind of local law enforceable at the suit

---

[8] See Chap. 22.

[9] See *Earl of Leicester* v. *Wells-next-the-Sea U.D.C.* [1973] Ch. 110.

[10] See *Drake* v. *Gray* [1936] Ch. 451; *Russell* v. *Archdale* [1964] Ch. 38.

of any plot-owner against any other plot-owner, irrespective of the dates on which they acquired their respective tenements. The main conditions were laid down in the leading case of *Elliston* v. *Reacher*.[11]

Discharge of restrictive covenants

There are various statutory provisions under which restrictive covenants may be discharged or modified. In particular, by the Law of Property Act 1925, s. 84, as amended by subsequent enactments, the Lands Tribunal has power to modify or discharge a restrictive covenant, with or without the payment of compensation, on various grounds set out in the section, *e.g.* that by reason of changes in the character of the neighbourhood or other circumstances the covenant has become obsolete or would impede some reasonable user of the land. In determining this question, the Tribunal is now authorised to have regard to the public interest and is required to take into account the development plan for the area.[12]

These provisions apply not only to freehold land but also to leaseholds if the lease was made for more than 40 years at least 25 of which have expired.

It should also be mentioned that if an action is brought to enforce a restrictive covenant and it would be inequitable to grant an injunction, *e.g.* by reason of the plaintiff's acquiescence in previous breaches of the covenant, the court may refuse to grant it.

(C) Superior Landlord and Sub-Tenant

If L grants a lease to T and T grants a sub-lease to ST, there is no privity of contract nor privity of estate between L and ST. L cannot, therefore, enforce the covenants in the head lease against ST under the principles which we have considered under (A) above. So far, however, as those covenants are restrictive, he may enforce them against ST under the doctrine of *Tulk* v. *Moxhay*. This is certainly so if those covenants were taken for the benefit of other land owned by the landlord, and apparently it is so even if the covenants were not so taken, because the landlord's reversion is a sufficient dominant tenement for this purpose.[13]

---

[11] [1908] 2 Ch. 665, C.A.; see also *Baxter* v. *Four Oaks Properties Ltd.* [1965] Ch. 654; *Re Dolphin's Conveyance* [1970] Ch. 654.
[12] Law of Property Act 1925, s. 84 (1A) (1B): these provisions were introduced by the Law of Property Act 1969.
[13] *Regent Oil Co. Ltd.* v. *J. A. Gregory (Hatch End) Ltd.* [1966] Ch. 402, C.A.

CHAPTER 19

MORTGAGES

A MORTGAGE of land is a transaction by which a borrower of money (the mortgagor) gives security for the loan to his lender (the mortgagee). The mortgagee then has certain rights against the land (*e.g.* a power of sale), by means of which he may raise any sums that become due to him from the borrower. He is not, therefore, restricted to a merely personal action against the borrower, although he does enjoy that right as well as his remedies against the land itself.

Most mortgages are of a legal estate in land—they are made by the freeholder or by a leaseholder. But a mortgage may be of an equitable interest in land. For example if land is settled on A for life with remainder to B in fee simple, it is possible for B to raise a loan of money by mortgaging his equitable interest in remainder under the settlement. It may be assumed that the discussion in the following pages is of mortgages of a legal estate unless the contrary is stated.

Methods of mortgaging

After 1925 if a mortgage is to be a legal mortgage it must be made by demise or by legal charge.[1] If a freehold is being mortgaged by demise the mortgagee will be given a long term of years (*i.e.* a long leasehold term), usually for 3,000 years, with a proviso for cesser on redemption, *i.e.* a proviso that the leasehold term is to cease when the mortgage is paid off. The corresponding method of mortgaging a leasehold is by sub-demise with a similar proviso—the mortgagee is given a sub-term (*i.e.* a sub-lease) for a term less by at least one day than that of the leasehold which is being mortgaged (in practice the sub-lease is usually for 10 days less than the leasehold mortgaged).

Both freeholds and leaseholds may be mortgaged by legal charge (or, to give it its full title, " charge by deed expressed to be made by way of legal mortgage "). The legal charge is an invention of the Law of Property Act 1925. Such a charge gives to the mortgagee the same rights and remedies as if he had a mortgage by demise or sub-demise, but does not technically give to him a term of years in the land. The legal charge has certain advantages over the mortgage by demise or sub-demise. For example, a mortgage of a leasehold created in this way will not be a breach of a tenant's covenant not to sub-let the premises, whereas a mortgage by sub-demise would be.

---

[1] Law of Property Act 1925, ss. 85 *et seq.*

It will be noticed that whichever method of mortgaging is adopted the mortgagor is left with a legal estate in the land. He may, therefore, create second and subsequent legal mortgages to secure any further loans that may be raised on the same land. The Law of Property Act 1925 prevents the creation of legal mortgages by any method other than those which have been described.

In the mortgage deed the mortgagor covenants to repay the principal money with interest on a date specified in the deed. This date is known as the legal (or contractual) date of redemption, and thereafter at common law the mortgagor has no right to redeem his property. Equity, however, compels the mortgagee to allow redemption at any time after the contractual date on tender to him of the " price of redemption," *i.e.* the principal money, arrears of interest [2] and the costs of discharging the mortgage. This equitable right of redemption, which arises once the contractual date has passed, was developed by equity into an equitable estate in the land, called the " equity of redemption," which the mortgagor is regarded as having from the moment of the execution of the mortgage deed. By reason of the existence of the equitable right of redemption it has become the practice to fix the contractual date of redemption very soon after (generally six months after) the date of execution of the mortgage.

An equitable mortgage of a legal estate in land may be made in one of two ways. First, a mortgage will not be a legal mortgage unless it is made by deed; but a mortgage which is not made by deed will be a valid equitable mortgage if either there is sufficient written evidence to satisfy the provisions of section 40 of the Law of Property Act 1925, or there have been sufficient acts of part performance.[3] Deposit of the title deeds with the mortgagee is a sufficient act of part performance, so that in theory a valid equitable mortgage can be made by a mere oral agreement between the parties supported by deposit of the title deeds. In practice a mortgagee usually insists upon having at least a written memorandum setting out the terms of the agreement. Temporary loans are often secured by deposit of title deeds accompanied by a " memorandum of deposit," as it is called. Secondly, even if a mortgage is created by deed, the mortgage will be merely an equitable mortgage if it does not show an intention to create a legal estate in the land. Quite commonly the memorandum of deposit to which reference has just been made is under seal, but this document does not create a legal mortgage because it does not show an intention to do so.

---

[2] *All* arrears must be paid, even though statute-barred; see *Holmes* v. *Cowcher* [1970] 1 W.L.R. 834, and p. 126, *post.*

[3] A further illustration of the doctrine discussed in Chap. 5.

A mortgage of an equitable interest in land (as opposed to an equitable mortgage of a legal estate) must be in writing.[4]

The equity of redemption

As we have seen, once the contractual date of redemption has passed, the mortgagor must rely upon his equitable right to redeem. Equity does not attach any time limit to the exercise of this right, but there are various events upon which the right will become extinguished. For example, if the mortgagee sells the land under his power of sale (the detail of which will be considered later),[5] the right will come to an end. Again, under the Limitation Act 1939, if the mortgagee takes possession of the land and remains in possession for 12 years without giving any acknowledgment of the mortgagor's title, the equitable right of redemption will become extinguished. As we shall see later,[6] equity itself, in foreclosure proceedings, may put a period to the equitable right of redemption.

Notice of intention to redeem

Equity has a maxim " he who seeks equity must do equity," and equity will not, therefore, allow the mortgagor to exercise his equitable right of redemption in an unconscionable manner. If the mortgagor were at liberty to repay the mortgage money without prior notice to the mortgagee, the mortgagee might have the money lying idle on his hands for a considerable time before finding a suitable new investment for it. Equity, therefore, requires the mortgagor to give reasonable prior notice to the mortgagee of his intention to exercise his equitable right of redemption, or pay additional interest instead. For a formal legal mortgage six months' notice will usually be required. The giving of notice or the payment of additional interest in lieu is not necessary if the mortgagee has already shown that he wants his money, e.g. by giving notice requiring repayment.

Consolidation

Another application of the principle " he who seeks equity must do equity " is in the doctrine of consolidation. In its simplest form this means that if the same person by separate mortgages mortgages two different properties to the same mortgagee, then seeks to exercise his equitable right to redeem one of the properties, the mortgagee can require him to redeem both or neither; otherwise the mortgagor might be able to redeem a property that was a more than adequate security for the loan made on it, leaving the mortgagee with a property that was an inadequate security for the loan made on that property. The

---

[4] Law of Property Act 1925, s. 53.
[5] See p. 112, *post.*
[6] See p. 114, *post.*

right to consolidate has been abolished by statute (now the Law of Property Act 1925, s. 93) unless the right is reserved in at least one of the mortgages: this is often done by providing expressly that section 93 shall not apply. Moreover, the right does not exist unless the contractual date of redemption has passed in both cases.

The right to consolidate exists not only in the simple case mentioned above, but also whenever the following conditions are satisfied:

(i) Both mortgages were made by the same mortgagor.

(ii) Either (a) the equities of redemption (*i.e.* the properties, subject to the mortgages thereon) are in one hand and the mortgages in another single hand, or (b) the position as at (a) has existed at some time in the past since when the equities of redemption have become separated.

The law was summarised in this sense in the leading case of *Pledge* v. *White* [7] in the House of Lords.

Example 1

A mortgages Blackacre to B.

A mortgages Whiteacre to C.

B and C transfer their mortgages to D.

If A then seeks to redeem one of the two properties, D can consolidate, *i.e.* can require A to pay off the mortgages on both properties or not redeem at all.

Rule (ii) above is here satisfied under (ii) (a).

Example 2

A mortgages Blackacre to B.

A mortgages Whiteacre to C.

A sells Blackacre, subject to the mortgage thereon, to X.

B and C transfer their mortgages to D.

If X or A seeks to redeem his property (Blackacre or Whiteacre, respectively) D cannot consolidate. Rule (ii) above is not satisfied because there has never been a moment of time when both the properties have been in one hand and both the mortgages in another single hand: the properties had become separated before the mortgages fell into one hand.

Example 3

A mortgages Blackacre to B.

A mortgages Whiteacre to B.

A sells Blackacre, subject to the mortgage thereon, to X.

If X or A seeks to redeem his property B can consolidate. Rule (ii) is satisfied under (ii) (b). It will be observed that in this case, as a condition of paying off the mortgage on his own property, X or A

[7] [1896] A.C. 187.

can be required to pay off the mortgage on the other property: that mortgage will not then be discharged, but will be transferred to the person making the payment off (*i.e.* X or A, as the case may be).[8]

Preserving the equity of redemption

Equity has evolved a series of rules for the protection of the equity of redemption. These rules are sometimes regarded as coming under the general principle " once a mortgage always a mortgage." They include the following:

(i) *The substance not the form*

Equity will treat as a mortgage any transaction that is in substance intended to give a security for the loan of money, whatever name the parties may give to the transaction. For example, if the lender of money insists upon the transaction being expressed as a conveyance on sale of the property to the lender, with an option to the borrower to re-purchase the property at an enhanced price within a certain time (the difference in price being in fact the interest on the loan), equity will treat this transaction as a mortgage in order that the mortgagor's right of redemption may be preserved: the mortgagor will then have the right to redeem even after the end of the fixed period specified in the deed.[9]

(ii) *Provisions repugnant to the equity of redemption*

Equity will treat as void any provision in the mortgage which would or might destroy the equity of redemption. For example, if the mortgage purports to give to the mortgagee an option to purchase the property, the grant of the option is void: otherwise by exercising the option the mortgagee could destroy the mortgagor's right of redemption.[10] Once the mortgage has been created, however, the mortgagor by an independent transaction may validly grant an option to purchase the property to the mortgagee.[11]

(iii) *Postponing the right of redemption*

Prima facie, in the absence of any evidence of fraud or oppression by the mortgagee, the parties can make what bargain they like as to the earliest possible date of redemption of the property [12]: they are not bound to follow the usual form, by which the contractual date of

---

[8] See p. 119, *post.*

[9] See *Barnhart* v. *Greenshields* (1853) 9 Moo.P.C. 18; *Waters* v. *Mynn* (1850) 15 L.T.(o.s.) 157.

[10] *Samuel* v. *Jarrah Timber Corporation* [1904] A.C. 323, in which Lord Macnaghten said (p. 326): " no one, I am sure, by the light of nature ever understood an English mortgage of real estate."

[11] *Reeve* v. *Lisle* [1902] A.C. 461.

[12] *Knightsbridge Estates Ltd.* v. *Byrne* [1939] Ch. 441 (affirmed on different grounds [1940] A.C. 613).

redemption is made six months after the date of the execution of the mortgage. But equity disallows a postponement which would render the right of redemption merely nominal or illusory, *e.g.* when a leasehold is mortgaged, a provision postponing the right of redemption until the lease itself has almost expired.[13] If a postponement is coupled with a " tie " between the mortgagor and the mortgagee which is void as being in restraint of trade,[14] it seems that the postponement will also be void, *e.g.* where the owner of a petrol station mortgages it to an oil company and agrees to take all his supplies from the company throughout the term of the mortgage, and not to redeem the mortgage for 21 years.[15]

(iv) *Other clogs on the equity of redemption*

Any provision in a mortgage is void to the extent that it would prevent the mortgagor on redemption from getting back his property in substantially the same condition as it was in when he mortgaged it. For example, if the owner of a free public-house (*i.e.* a public-house the owner of which is at liberty to sell any brewer's beers) mortgages it to a brewer, any provision in the mortgage requiring the mortgagor to sell only the mortgagee's beers will be void so far as the restriction purports to continue after the mortgagor has paid off the loan : otherwise having mortgaged a free public-house he would get back a tied one.[16]

(v) *Collateral advantages*

In the absence of evidence of fraud or oppression by the mortgagee, equity has no objection to a provision in the mortgage giving to the mortgagee some collateral advantage, *i.e.* some advantage over and above repayment of the loan with interest.[17] Thus, there is no objection to a provision in the mortgage of a free public-house which requires the mortgagor to sell only the mortgagee's beers *so long as the mortgage lasts*.[18] But if the advantage operates as a clog on, or is repugnant to, the equity of redemption, it will be void. Thus, if the mortgage provides that the property can only be redeemed on payment of a premium, and the amount of the premium is excessive, equity will allow the mortgagor to redeem on repaying the principal plus a reasonable rate of interest.[19]

---

[13] *Fairclough* v. *Swan Brewery Co. Ltd.* [1912] A.C. 565.
[14] This is a common law doctrine based on grounds of public policy.
[15] *Esso Petroleum Co. Ltd.* v. *Harper's Garage (Stourport) Ltd.* [1968] A.C. 269.
[16] *Noakes & Co. Ltd.* v. *Rice* [1902] A.C. 24.
[17] *Kreglinger (G. & C.)* v. *New Patagonia Meat and Cold Storage Co. Ltd.* [1914] A.C. 25.
[18] *Biggs* v. *Hoddinott* [1898] 2 Ch. 307. But note the *Esso* case, *ante.*
[19] *Cityland and Property (Holdings)* v. *Dabrah* [1968] Ch. 166.

Mortgagee's remedies

In addition to his right to sue the mortgagor personally for any money that becomes due to him, the mortgagee has (or may have) the following main remedies: a right to take possession of the land; a right of sale; a right to appoint a receiver of the rents and profits of the land; and a right to foreclose. Each of these main remedies must be considered separately.

(i) *Possession*

From the moment that a mortgage is created, a legal mortgagee, and perhaps an equitable mortgagee, has the right to take possession of the land. By this means the mortgagee can obtain the rents and profits of the land and can, if necessary, himself grant leases of the land (as we shall see hereafter).[20] A mortgagee will not, of course, normally exercise this right except either as a preliminary to selling the property, or as a means of recovering interest on the mortgage debt; and in either case it will usually be necessary for him to bring an *action* for possession against the mortgagor. If the mortgage is of a dwelling-house, the court now has power to adjourn such proceedings or to suspend or postpone the possession order, if it appears that the mortgagor is likely within a reasonable period to pay the amount due or remedy any other default.[21]

Any sums received by a mortgagee in possession must, of course, be set off against the mortgage debt; furthermore, a mortgagee who does take possession is accountable to the mortgagor on the footing of wilful default: he is chargeable, not only with any profits that he does make, but also for any further profits that he ought to have made. For example, if the property is a free public-house and the mortgagee is a brewer, and the mortgagee takes possession of the premises and then grants a lease of them containing a term which requires the lessee to sell only the mortgagee's beers, the mortgagee will be accountable to the mortgagor for the higher rent he could have obtained if he had let the premises without any such tie.[22] By reason of this strict accountability, a mortgagee will generally prefer to appoint a receiver of the rents and profits rather than himself take possession: he will not then be accountable in this way.

(ii) *Sale*

The two principal statutory remedies are the power of sale and the power to appoint a receiver. Both are given by the Law of Property

---

[20] See p. 115, *post.*
[21] Administration of Justice Act 1970, ss. 36–39. The Administration of Justice Act 1973, s. 8, extends this power to cases where the mortgagor appears likely to bring payment of instalments up to date.
[22] *White* v. *City of London Brewery Co.* (1889) 42 Ch.D. 237.

Act 1925, s. 101, to every mortgagee whose mortgage is by deed. Thus every legal mortgagee has these powers, and an equitable mortgagee enjoys them if his mortgage is by deed, *e.g.* if it was created by deposit of title deeds accompanied by a memorandum of deposit under seal.

The power of sale *arises* as soon as the contractual date for redemption has passed. But it does not become *exercisable* until one of three events occurs: (i) the mortgagee has served notice requiring payment of the mortgage money and default has been made in payment for three months after such service; (ii) some interest is in arrear and unpaid for two months after becoming due; or (iii) there has been a breach of some provision contained in the mortgage deed or in the Act which is to be observed by the mortgagor, other than a covenant for payment of the principal money or interest thereon.

The purchaser from the mortgagee is concerned to see that the power of sale has arisen, but he is not concerned to verify that it has become exercisable; he will get a good title even if it has not,[23] but the mortgagee will then be liable in damages to the mortgagor.

When the mortgagee of a freehold sells the land under his statutory power of sale he conveys to the purchaser the fee simple vested in the mortgagor, free from any subsequent (but not prior) mortgages. Similarly, when the mortgagee of a leasehold sells, he (in general) conveys to the mortgagee the leasehold term vested in the mortgagor free from any subsequent mortgages.[24] After paying off what is due to himself the mortgagee holds any surplus proceeds of sale upon trust for any subsequent mortgagee, and subject thereto for the mortgagor.[25]

The statutory power of sale may be varied or extended by the mortgage.

A mortgagee is not a trustee of his statutory power of sale and need not exert himself to get the best price obtainable (there is an exception in the case of building societies). However, the mortgagee must not deliberately sell at a lower price than he can readily obtain, and he must make a genuine sale: thus he may not sell to himself, directly or indirectly, whether by private treaty or at public auction. Furthermore, the mortgagee is under a duty of care in exercising his power of sale, and may be liable in damages if through his negligence the property is sold for less than it ought to have realised.[26]

A mortgagee whose mortgage is not by deed does not enjoy the benefit of the statutory power of sale. But the court may order a sale upon application by him (or anyone interested in the equity

---

[23] Law of Property Act 1925, s. 104.
[24] *Ibid.* ss. 88, 89.
[25] *Ibid.* s. 105.
[26] *Cuckmere Brick Co. Ltd.* v. *Mutual Finance Ltd.* [1971] Ch. 949.

of redemption, *e.g.* the mortgagor).[27] An equitable mortgagee, on the other hand, does enjoy the statutory power if his mortgage is by deed. He cannot, however, pass a legal estate to the purchaser unless there is some conveyancing device in the mortgage which enables him to do this, *e.g.* an irrevocable power of attorney given by the mortgagor to the mortgagee for this purpose.

(iii) *Receiver*

A mortgagee whose mortgage is by deed has statutory power to appoint a receiver of the income of the mortgaged property as soon as the contractual date for redemption has passed.[28] The Law of Property Act,[29] however, directs that he shall not do so until the power of sale has become exercisable. Such a receiver is deemed to be the agent of the mortgagor, who, therefore, is to be solely responsible for the receiver's acts or defaults unless the mortgage otherwise provides.[30] It is for this reason that a mortgagee who wishes to obtain the profits of the land will generally prefer to appoint a receiver rather than take possession of the land himself: if he appoints a receiver he escapes liability on the footing of wilful default.[31] After paying various outgoings and his own commission the receiver is to apply money received by him in payment of the interest accruing due under the mortgage, and, if so directed in writing by the mortgagee, in or towards discharge of the principal money. The residue is to be paid by him to the person who but for the possession of the receiver would have been entitled to receive the income [32]: this is normally the mortgagor.

This power also may be varied or extended by the mortgage.

A mortgagee whose mortgage is not by deed may apply to the court for the appointment of a receiver.

(iv) *Foreclosure*

As soon as the contractual date for redemption has passed, the mortgagee may start foreclosure proceedings in the courts. In such proceedings the court will make a foreclosure order nisi in the first instance, giving to the mortgagor a fixed period (usually six months) within which he must redeem the property, failing which the order will be made absolute, the mortgagor will lose his right of redemption and the mortgagee will become beneficial owner of the property.[33]

---

[27] Law of Property Act 1925, s. 91.
[28] *Ibid.* s. 101.
[29] s. 109.
[30] *Ibid.*
[31] See p. 112, *ante.*
[32] Law of Property Act 1925, s. 109.
[33] The court has power to order sale instead of foreclosure (*ibid.* s. 91 (2)).

By this equitable remedy of foreclosure equity takes away from the mortgagor that which it itself has created, *viz.* the equity of redemption: foreclosure, therefore, is the mortgagee's counterblast to the mortgagor's equity of redemption. A foreclosure order absolute vests the mortgagor's legal estate in the mortgagee, free from any subsequent mortgages. If there are subsequent mortgages, each subsequent mortgagee must be given the right to pay off the plaintiff's mortgage and take a transfer of it, failing which the subsequent mortgagee will lose his security when the order absolute is made. Prior mortgages are unaffected and remain attached to the land.

In exceptional circumstances the court on application may reopen the foreclosure, even though an order absolute has been made, *i.e.* the court may restore to the mortgagor his equity of redemption. Moreover, the foreclosure will automatically be re-opened if the mortgagee after foreclosure absolute sues the mortgagor on the mortgage debt. For this reason if a mortgagee who has obtained a foreclosure order absolute sells the property he cannot thereafter sue the mortgagor on the mortgage debt: he is not in a position to allow the mortgagor to redeem the property. With this exception a mortgagee's remedies are cumulative, *i.e.* the fact that he has exercised one of the remedies does not prevent him from making use of another if he has not obtained complete redress.

The equitable remedy of foreclosure is available to all mortgagees, legal or equitable.

The power of leasing

The Law of Property Act 1925, s. 99, gives power to grant leases of mortgaged land which will be binding upon all persons interested therein. The power is given to the mortgagor, unless the mortgagee has taken possession or has appointed a receiver, in which case the power belongs to him. A mortgagee who has appointed a receiver may delegate the power of leasing to the receiver. The leases which the section authorises are agricultural or occupation leases for any term not exceeding 50 years, and building leases for any term not exceeding 999 years. The lease must reserve the best rent that can reasonably be obtained, and no fine may be taken, and other conditions are laid down by the Act.

With the exception of mortgages of agricultural land,[34] the statutory power of leasing can be excluded by the mortgage, and in practice the mortgagor's power is commonly excluded. The statutory power may also be extended by the mortgage.

---

[34] Agricultural Holdings Act 1948, Sched. 7.

Quite apart from the statutory power, if either party to the mortgage grants a lease, that lease will be binding upon him, although not upon the other party to the mortgage.

Priority of successive mortgages

(a) *Mortgages of a legal estate*

Where several mortgages of the same land have been created successively, and the security proves inadequate, the question of the priority of those mortgages arises, *i.e.* of the order in which effect will be given to the rights of the several mortgagees. The general rule is " first in time first in right," *i.e.* priority follows the order in which the mortgages were created. Apart from cases where the title to the land is registered under the Land Registration Act 1925,[35] there are two main exceptions to this general rule. To understand these it is first necessary to notice that if a mortgage is protected by deposit of title deeds with the mortgagee it is not registrable under the Land Charges Act 1972, but if it is not so protected then it is registrable under the Act—if it is a legal mortgage it is registrable as a " puisne mortgage "; if it is an equitable mortgage it is registrable as a " general equitable charge." We may now consider the two exceptions.

(i) If mortgage no. 1 is an equitable mortgage protected by deposit (and so not registrable) and mortgage no. 2 is a legal mortgage, and the legal mortgagee took his mortgage in good faith and without notice, actual or constructive, of the equitable mortgage, the legal mortgage will rank first. This is not because of any misconduct on the part of the equitable mortgagee, but because, as we have seen,[36] an equitable interest does not bind a subsequent bona fide purchaser for value of a legal estate without notice of the equitable interest. The position of the earlier equitable mortgagee is not, however, as precarious as might at first sight appear, because the fact that the title deeds have been deposited with him will ordinarily ensure that the legal mortgagee has notice, actual or constructive, of the equitable mortgage: if the legal mortgagee inquires for the title deeds he will generally discover the existence of the equitable mortgage, and if he does not inquire for the deeds he will be fixed with constructive notice of that mortgage. But if the legal mortgagee did inquire for the title deeds and the mortgagor gave a false, but credible, explanation of his inability to produce them, the legal mortgagee would not be fixed with notice of the equitable mortgage, and he would have priority.

(ii) If mortgage no. 1 (whether legal or equitable) is not protected by deposit and it is not registered before the creation of mortgage

---

[35] See Chap. 22.
[36] See Chap. 5.

no. 2, mortgage no. 2 will have priority. The failure to register mortgage no. 1 rendered it void against a subsequent " purchaser " of the land, and the subsequent mortgagee (whether legal or equitable) is within the definition of " purchaser." [37] In such a case the later purchaser has priority, even if he had actual notice of the existence of the unregistered interest. It is possible that an exception to this rule is created by the Law of Property Act 1925, s. 97, which provides that a registrable mortgage shall rank according to the date of its registration as a land charge. It may, therefore, be that, where two successive mortgages are both registrable, the first mortgage will rank first if it was registered first, even if it was not registered when the second mortgage was executed. This apparent conflict between the Land Charges Act 1972 and the Law of Property Act 1925 has not yet been resolved by the courts.

It will be observed that, so far as the Land Charges Act is concerned, if the second mortgage is registrable nothing turns upon *its* registration, because failure to register a registrable interest merely renders it void against a *later* purchaser: its priority in relation to an earlier mortgage would not be affected by its non-registration.

When the title to the land itself is registered under the Land Registration Act 1925, the priority of successive mortgages of the land generally follows the order in which the requisite entries relating to the mortgages are entered on the register.

(b) *Mortgages of an equitable interest*

The priority of successive mortgages of an equitable interest in any property, real or personal, is governed by the rule in *Dearle* v. *Hall*,[38] as amended by the Law of Property Act 1925, s. 137. Under this rule priority generally follows the order in which the respective mortgagees give written notice of their mortgages to the trustees of the settlement or trust under which the mortgaged interest subsists. For example, if by means of a strict settlement, or a trust for sale, land is settled on A for life with remainder to B in fee simple (or absolutely), and B mortgages his equitable remainder first to X and then to Y, the priority of the two mortgages will generally follow the order in which X and Y give written notice of their mortgages to the trustees of the settlement or trust for sale: the first to give notice will rank first. As an exception, if when Y took his mortgage he had actual or constructive notice of the existence of X's mortgage Y cannot gain priority by being the first to give notice: it would be fraudulent for him to claim priority in those circumstances.[39]

---

[37] See Chap. 22.
[38] (1823) 3 Russ. 1.
[39] *Re Holmes* (1885) 29 Ch.D. 786.

It should be noted that mortgages of a beneficial interest under a settlement or trust for sale are not registrable under the Land Charges Act 1972, nor is priority affected by deposit of documents of title.

Tacking

Sometimes the rules of priority are affected by the doctrine of tacking. After 1925 only one form of tacking is permitted, namely the tacking of further advances, which is now regulated by the Law of Property Act 1925, s. 94. If two successive mortgages of the same land are made to A and B, respectively, and A then makes a further loan to the borrower on the same security, A may sometimes tack (*i.e.* add) this further advance to his original loan, and so claim priority for both his loans over B's mortgage. A prior mortgagee has the right to tack thus in three cases—(i) if an arrangement has been made to that effect with the intervening mortgagee; (ii) if he had no notice of the intervening mortgage at the time when he made the further advance; (iii) whether or not he had such notice, if his mortgage imposed upon him an obligation to make the further advance. It will be observed that in case (ii) (the ordinary case), notice of the intervening mortgage will be fatal to the right to tack. In general, if the intervening mortgage was registered under the Land Charges Act 1972 at the date of the further advance, the registration will constitute sufficient notice to prevent tacking. There is an exception to this rule: if the prior mortgage was made expressly for securing a current account or other further advances (though without imposing an obligation to make such advances), registration under the Land Charges Act is not sufficient notice to prevent the prior mortgagee from tacking (unless he actually searched the register). But the prior mortgagee cannot tack if when he made his further advance he had actual notice of the intervening mortgage. For this reason when a first mortgage is expressly made to secure a current account or other further advances that may be made, a second mortgagee should always give express notice of his mortgage to the earlier mortgagee: by so doing he prevents tacking.

Discharge of mortgages

If a mortgage has been created by demise or sub-demise, all that is required, in theory, to discharge the mortgage is an ordinary receipt for the mortgage money, because by the Law of Property Act 1925, ss. 5 and 116, the mortgagee's term of years will thereupon become a satisfied term and will cease. In practice, however, reliance is placed, not upon these provisions, but upon a receipt endorsed on or annexed to the mortgage which complies with the provisions of section 115 of the Act. Under this section such a receipt, if it states the name of the

MORTGAGES 119

person who pays the money and is signed by the mortgagee, will operate to discharge (or " vacate ") any mortgage. An endorsed receipt will not vacate the mortgage, however, but will (with certain exceptions) transfer it to the person making the payment if that person is not the person entitled to the immediate equity of redemption.⁴⁰

⁴⁰ See p. 110, *ante*.

CHAPTER 20

DISABILITIES

Infants [1]

AFTER 1925 an infant cannot hold a legal estate in land, although he may in general own other property, including an equitable interest in land. Land which is held upon trust for an infant for an estate in fee simple or for a term of years absolute is settled land for the purposes of the Settled Land Act 1925, s. 1.[2] The legal estate must be vested in the statutory owner by vesting deed or assent, and the beneficial entitlement of the infant will be declared by the trust instrument. The statutory owner has all the powers of disposition of a tenant for life under the Act; the infancy of the person who is beneficially entitled does not, therefore, prevent a binding disposition of the land from being made, and this is why the Act makes the land settled land —an infant cannot make a binding disposition of property which is vested in him,[3] and it is the policy of the 1925 Acts to keep land alienable at all times.

A purported conveyance of a legal estate in land to an infant alone, or to two or more persons jointly both or all of whom are infants, for his or their own benefit, operates only as an agreement for valuable consideration (whether such consideration has in fact been given or not) to execute a settlement by means of a vesting deed and a trust instrument in favour of the infant or infants, and in the meantime to hold the land in trust for the infant or infants.[4] A conveyance of a legal estate in land to an infant jointly with one or more other persons of full age operates to vest the legal estate in the other person or persons on the statutory trusts,[5] i.e. upon the trust to sell the land and to hold the net rents and profits pending sale, and net proceeds of sale after sale, upon trust for the person or persons of full age and the infant: the beneficial interest of the infant is, therefore, preserved.

The appointment of an infant as trustee of any property is void.[6] The appointment of an infant as executor is not void, but is suspended

---

[1] As from January 1, 1970, an infant (or minor) is a person below the age of 18 years (not, as previously, 21 years) (Family Law Reform Act 1969, ss. 1, 12).

[2] See p. 48, *ante*.

[3] Such dispositions are voidable by the infant during minority or within a reasonable time of attaining majority.

[4] Settled Land Act 1925, s. 27.

[5] Law of Property Act 1925, s. 19.

[6] *Ibid*. s. 20.

during his minority [7]: other arrangements are then made for the administration of the deceased's estate to be undertaken during the minority, but the infant is entitled to a grant of probate on attaining majority.

There are special provisions with regard to infants as mortgagees.[8]

A curious provision of the Administration of Estates Act 1925, s. 51 (3), enacts that if an infant dies without having married and entitled at his death to a vested equitable interest in fee simple in land, or to an absolute interest in property settled to devolve with such land or as freehold land, he shall be deemed to have had an entailed interest in the property. In the result, the land upon the infant's death reverts to the grantor (*i.e.* the person who gave the land to the infant) or, if he is dead, his estate, because the notional entail comes to an end.

Persons Suffering from Mental Disorder

Under the Mental Health Act 1959 the court has wide powers of disposition over the property of a person who is suffering from mental disorder and may appoint a receiver to exercise these powers on its behalf. So long as a receivership is in force the patient has no power to make an *inter vivos* disposition of his property, although he may make a valid will during a lucid interval. If no receiver has been appointed, the position with regard to a disposition of his property by a person suffering from mental disorder is as follows:

(i) It is *valid* if the disposition is made for valuable consideration and the other party has no notice of the disability.

(ii) It is *voidable* if it is made for valuable consideration and the other party has notice of the disability.

(iii) It is *void* if the disposition is gratuitous.

Other Persons and Bodies

Married women, traitors and felons, aliens, corporations and charities were all formerly subject to particular disabilities, but with slight exceptions these disabilities have now been abolished by various statutes. A few vestiges remain, *e.g.* a charity may not even now dispose of land which forms part of its endowment without special permission, unless the charity is one of a number of privileged charities which are exempt from the restriction.

---

[7] Judicature Act 1925, s. 165.
[8] Law of Property Act 1925, s. 19.

CHAPTER 21

LIMITATION

THE Limitation Act 1939 contains provisions under which an action to recover possession of land must be brought within a certain time. The basic provision is contained in section 4 of the Act, which provides that no action shall be brought by any person to recover any land after the expiration of 12 years [1] from the date on which the right of action accrued to him or, if it first accrued to some person through whom he claims, the date when it accrued to that person. In the ordinary case the right of action accrues when the person in possession (hereafter called " the former owner ") is dispossessed by another person (hereafter called " the squatter ").[2] The net result of these provisions is that if the former owner is to recover the land he must bring his action against the squatter within 12 years from the date when he was dispossessed by the squatter.

It is comparatively rare for one person actively to dispossess another. Dispossession is most likely to occur when there is a genuine misunderstanding as to the correct boundaries of land and one person takes possession of part of another's land believing it to be his own.

Future interests

If a succession of interests subsists in land and adverse possession is taken during a preceding interest, the owner of a future interest may generally bring an action to recover the land within 12 years from the date when adverse possession was taken or six years from the date when his future interest fell into possession, whichever period last expires.[3] For example, if land is settled on A for life with remainder to B in fee simple, and adverse possession of the land is taken by a squatter during A's life interest, when A dies B may bring an action against the squatter within 12 years from the date when the squatter took possession of the land or six years from the death of A, whichever is the longer. This special rule has no application if adverse possession has been taken before the future interest is created. For example, in the above illustration if adverse possession had been taken by the squatter before the land was settled on A and B neither A nor B could bring an action to recover the land from the squatter after the expiration of 12 years from the date when the squatter took

---

[1] 30 years when the action is brought by the Crown or a spiritual or eleemosynary corporation sole (60 years for actions by the Crown to recover *foreshore*).
[2] ss. 5, 10.
[3] s. 6.

possession, because the settlor, through whom each would claim, would himself then be barred. Moreover, there are the following exceptions to the general rule:

(i) The special rule has no application to the owner of an interest which falls into possession on the determination of an entailed interest. For example, if land is settled on A in tail with remainder to B in fee simple, and S takes adverse possession of the land during the currency of the entailed interest, B must bring his action within 12 years from the date when adverse possession was taken. Yet B cannot sue until his remainder falls into possession, so that he may well be barred by the Act before he has any chance to sue.

(ii) Where a person is entitled to an interest in possession and at the same time he is also entitled to a future interest in the same land, and his right to recover the interest in possession becomes barred under the Act, no action may be brought by that person or by any person claiming through him in respect of the future interest unless in the meantime possession of the land has been recovered by a person entitled to an intermediate interest. For example, if land is settled on A for life with remainder to B for life with remainder to A in fee simple, and S takes possession of the land and holds it for 12 years during A's lifetime, no action can be brought by A's personal representatives in respect of the fee simple remainder unless after A's death possession of the land has been recovered by B.

Leaseholds generally

(i) If a squatter takes possession of land after a lease of it has been granted, the landlord may sue the squatter to recover the land within 12 years after the determination of the lease. For example, if shortly after the fee simple owner has granted a lease for 50 years to a tenant a squatter takes possession of the land and holds it for 12 years, the tenant becomes statute-barred, so that the squatter will be entitled to remain in possession of the land for the rest of the lease; but the fee simple owner will have 12 years from the determination of the lease within which to sue the squatter for recovery of the land.

(ii) A lessee under a lease for a fixed term cannot acquire a squatter's title against his own landlord by virtue of his possession of the land during the currency of the lease. If, for example, shortly after a lease for 50 years has been granted the lessee begins to withhold payment of his rent and continues to do so for 12 years, he does not thereby acquire a squatter's title against his landlord. The landlord at any time may require the tenant to pay rent for the remainder of the leasehold term. He may also sue the tenant for arrears of rent so far as the Act allows: he may generally recover up to six years' arrears by action or distress,[4] but in the case of agricultural holdings the right of *distress* is limited to one year's rent.[5]

(iii) If a tenant holds over at the end of a lease without the landlord's consent he becomes a tenant at sufferance.[6] The landlord then has 12 years from the determination of the lease within which to sue the tenant for recovery of the land.

(iv) If a person wrongfully claims to be entitled to the reversion upon a written lease (other than a tenancy at will or a lease granted by the Crown) and demands payment of the rent, being a rent of at least £1 per annum, from the tenant and the tenant pays the rent to that person for 12 years, the person to whom the rent has been paid acquires a squatter's title to the reversion.[7]

Tenancies at will [8]

The Act provides that a tenancy at will shall for the purposes of the Act be deemed to be determined at the expiration of one year from the commencement of the tenancy, unless the tenancy has been previously determined, and that accordingly the right of action of the person entitled to the land shall be deemed to have accrued on the date of such determination.[9] The effect of this is that if a tenant at will remains in possession of the land for 13 years after the commencement of the tenancy (or 12 years after the tenancy is actually determined if that period is shorter), the tenant acquires a squatter's title against his landlord. If, however, before the landlord becomes statute-barred the tenant pays rent to the landlord, or gives to him a written acknowledgment of his title, the 12-year period will begin to run afresh.

Periodical tenancies

The Act provides [10] that a tenancy from year to year or for any other period not granted in writing shall for the purposes of the Act be deemed to be determined at the expiration of the first year or other period of the tenancy, and that accordingly the right of action of the person entitled to the land shall be deemed to have accrued at the date of such determination or on the date of the last receipt of rent.[11] If, for example, a tenant under a yearly tenancy which has not been granted in writing remains in possession without paying rent for

---

[4] s. 17.
[5] Agricultural Holdings Act 1948, s. 18.
[6] See p. 30, *ante.*
[7] Limitation Act 1939, ss. 9, 10.
[8] Distinguish a mere licence: a licensee cannot acquire title by adverse possession (*Cobb* v. *Lane* [1952] 1 All E.R. 1199; *Hughes* v. *Griffin* [1969] 1 W.L.R. 23).
[9] s. 9.
[10] *Ibid.*
[11] See *Hayward* v. *Challoner* [1968] 1 Q.B. 107 (C.A.).

13 years from the commencement of the tenancy, he will acquire a squatter's title against the landlord. Here again, however, the payment of rent or the giving of a written acknowledgment of the landlord's title before the landlord becomes barred will start the 12-year period running afresh.

If a periodical tenancy is granted in writing time does not begin to run against the landlord until the tenancy is determined.

Rentcharges

The Act [12] defines land as including rentcharges and provides more specifically that in relation to rentcharges references in the Act to the possession of land shall be construed as references to the receipt of the rent, and references to the date of dispossession of land shall be construed as references to the date of the last receipt of rent. In consequence of these provisions if a rentcharge is unpaid for 12 years the rentcharge becomes extinguished. Moreover, if a person wrongfully claims to be entitled to the rentcharge and the rent is paid to him for 12 years, the former owner of the rentcharge becomes statute-barred and the claimant acquires a squatter's title to the rentcharge.

Mortgages

Both the mortgagor's right of redemption, and the mortgagee's rights to recover principal and interest and to foreclose, may be extinguished by lapse of time.[13]

(a) Right of redemption

As has already been seen,[14] when a mortgagee of land has been in possession of the mortgaged land for a period of 12 years no action to redeem the land of which the mortgagee has been so in possession shall thereafter be brought by the mortgagor or any person claiming through him. The Act does not apply to an action to redeem pure personalty, and there is no fixed period wherein such an action must be brought by the mortgagor; but the action may be barred by laches, *i.e.* such delay as renders it inequitable for the action to be brought.

(b) Rights of mortgagee

The Act provides [15] that no action shall be brought to recover any principal sum of money secured by a mortgage on any property, real or personal, after the expiration of 12 years from the date when the right to receive the money accrued (*i.e.* the contractual date of redemption).

---

[12] s. 31.
[13] As to the effect of acknowledgment and part payment, see p. 127, *post.*
[14] See p. 108, *ante.*
[15] s. 18.

A foreclosure action in respect of mortgaged land must be brought within 12 years from the date when the right to foreclose accrued (*i.e.* the contractual date of redemption). A foreclosure action in respect of pure personalty which has been mortgaged must be brought before the expiration of 12 years from the date on which the right to foreclose accrued, except that if after that date the mortgagee has been in possession of the mortgaged propery, the right to foreclose is not deemed to have accrued until the date on which the mortgagee's possession discontinued.

The Act also provides that the right to receive any principal money secured by a mortgage and the right to foreclose shall not be deemed to accrue so long as the property comprises any future interest or any life insurance policy which has not matured or been determined.[16]

As regards the interest payable under a mortgage, the general rule is that a mortgagee may not recover more than six years' arrears, but special provision is made for cases where a prior mortgagee has been in possession of the property charged and cases where the property subject to the mortgage comprises a future interest or life insurance policy and it is a term of the mortgage that arrears of interest are to be treated as part of the principal sum: interest is not then deemed to become due before the right to receive the principal has accrued.[17]

Settled land and land held on trust

The provisions of the Act are applied [18] to equitable interests in land including interests in the proceeds of sale of land held upon trust for sale, in like manner as they apply to legal estates, and accordingly a right of action to recover the land is, for the purposes of the Act, deemed to accrue to a person entitled in possession to such an equitable interest in the same way as it would have accrued if his interest had been a legal estate in the land. However, the title of a tenant for life or statutory owner of settled land to the legal estate is not to be extinguished so long as the right of action to recover the land of any person entitled to a beneficial interest has not accrued or has not been barred by the Act. Similarly, when land is held upon trust, including a trust for sale, the right of the trustees is not to be extinguished so long as the right of action to recover the land of any beneficiary has not accrued or has not been barred. For example, if land is settled on A for life with remainder to B in fee simple, and S takes adverse possession of the land and holds it for 12 years during A's lifetime, A's right to the beneficial life interest will become

[16] s. 18.
[17] *Ibid.*
[18] By s. 7.

extinguished, but his title to the legal estate (vested in him as the " tenant for life " of the Settled Land Act) will not, because no cause of action has yet accrued to the remainderman B.

The Act also provides [19] that possession of settled land, or land held on trust for sale, by a beneficiary who is not solely and absolutely entitled shall not bar the title of a tenant for life, statutory owner, or trustee, or of any other beneficiary. Moreover, trustees cannot acquire a squatter's title against their own beneficiaries.[20] A somewhat curious consequence of these provisions is that, as co-ownership of land now involves a statutory trust for sale,[21] one co-owner cannot, by ousting his fellows, acquire a squatter's title to the land [22]: he will be a beneficiary under the trust for sale and often a trustee as well.

Disabilities

If on the date when a right of action accrues, for which a period of limitation is prescribed by the Act, the person to whom it accrues is under disability (infancy or unsoundness of mind), the action may be brought at any time before the expiration of six years from the date when the person ceased to be under disability or died, whichever event first occurred, notwithstanding that the period of limitation has expired.[23] There is a proviso that no action to recover land or money charged on land shall be brought after the expiration of 30 years from the date on which the right of action accrued. It will be observed that the section applies only if the disability subsists at the date of the accrual of the cause of action, otherwise there is no extension of time for disability.

When a right of action which has accrued to a person under disability accrues on the death of that person while still under disability to another person who is under disability, no further extension of time shall be allowed by reason of the disability of the second person.[24] Successive disabilities without a break of the *same* person, however, rank as one disability, *e.g.* where A is an infant at the date of the accrual of the cause of action to him and he becomes of unsound mind before attaining his majority.

Acknowledgment and part-payment

Where there has accrued a right of action (including a foreclosure action) to recover land, or any right of a mortgagee of pure personalty to bring a foreclosure action in respect of the property, and the person

---

[19] s. 7.
[20] s. 19.
[21] See Chap. 11.
[22] *Re Landi* [1939] Ch. 828.
[23] s. 22.
[24] *Ibid.*

in possession of the property acknowledges the title of the person to whom the right of action has accrued, or in the case of an action by a mortgagee the person in possession makes any payment in respect of the mortgage debt, whether of principal or interest, the right shall be deemed to have accrued on and not before the date of the acknowledgment or payment.[25] For example, if a mortgagor in possession of the mortgaged land makes a payment of interest to the mortgagee, the mortgagee may bring a foreclosure action within 12 years from the date of that payment: he is not limited to 12 years from the contracual date of redemption, as would otherwise have been the case.

Where a mortgagee is by virtue of the mortgage in possession of the mortgaged land, and he either receives a sum in respect of the principal or interest of the mortgage debt or he acknowledges the title of the mortgagor, an action to redeem the land may be brought at any time before the expiration of 12 years from the date of the payment or acknowledgment.[26]

For the above purposes an acknowledgment must be in writing and signed by the person making the acknowledgment. Any such acknowledgment, and any such payment as has been mentioned, may be made by the agent of the person by whom it is required to be made and shall be made to the person whose title or claim is being acknowledged or his agent.[27] There are detailed provisions [28] as to the effect of acknowledgment or part-payment on persons other than the maker or recipient, *e.g.* where one of two or more mortgagees in possession gives an acknowledgment of the mortgagor's title.

Once the right of a person to bring an action to recover land has become barred under the Act the title of that person to the land is extinguished.[29] It follows that no acknowledgment or payment given or made thereafter will revive his right to recover the land.

Fraud

Where in the case of any action for which a period of limitation is prescribed by the Act the action is based upon the fraud of the defendant or his agent (or any person through whom he claims or his agent), or the right of action is concealed by the fraud of any such person, the period of limitation shall not begin to run until the plaintiff has discovered the fraud or could with reasonable diligence have discovered it. This provision has, however, no application to an action against a bona fide purchaser for value of property who was not a party to the fraud and did not at the time of the purchase know or have reason to believe that any fraud had been committed.[30]

---

[25] s. 23.   [26] *Ibid.*
[27] s. 24.   [28] In s. 25.
[29] s. 16.   [30] s. 26.

The nature of the squatter's title

Possession of land of itself gives a better right to the land than that of anyone else except a person who can prove a better title to it. It follows that if the only person who can prove a better title to the land is statute-barred, the possession gives a title to the land which is good against the whole world. It is upon this principle that the squatter's title depends: there is no transfer, notional or otherwise, of the title of the former owner to the squatter. Thus the squatter is not a purchaser for value of the land and cannot claim to be entitled as such to take free from equitable interests (such as restrictive covenants) of which he has no notice.[31] Again, if a squatter takes possession of land which has been let under a lease and acquires a good squatter's title against the lessee, the landlord cannot directly sue the squatter upon the tenant's covenants in the lease [32]; but if the landlord has a right to re-enter for breach of the tenant's covenants in the lease the squatter may deem it wise to perform those covenants in order to escape ouster by the landlord,[33] and, if the lease provides for payment of a reduced rent if the tenant performs the tenant's covenants in the lease, and the squatter chooses to pay rent at the reduced rate, he will then be estopped from denying his liability on the other covenants in the lease.[34] It also follows that if a squatter obtains a squatter's title against a lessee, and the lessee thereupon acquires the reversion, he can at once oust the squatter: the lease has become merged in the reversion, by virtue of his ownership of which the former tenant is now claiming possession.[35] Equally, if in similar circumstances the tenant surrenders the lease to his landlord, the landlord can at once oust the squatter.[36]

Even before a squatter's title has been acquired, one who takes possession of another's land at once acquires an interest in it which he can assign *inter vivos* or dispose of by his will, and which will pass to his statutory next of kin on his intestacy. Moreover, if a squatter is himself ousted by another squatter, the second squatter, in defending an action brought by the former owner of the land, can add to his own period of possession that of the squatter whom he has ousted. Presumably, however, the first squatter could recover the land from the second squatter if he brought an action against him

---

[31] *Re Nisbet and Potts' Contract* [1906] 1 Ch. 386.

[32] *Tichborne* v. *Weir* (1892) 67 L.T. 735.

[33] A squatter has no claim to relief against forfeiture (*Tickner* v. *Buzzacott* [1965] Ch. 426).

[34] *Ashe* v. *Hogan* [1920] I.R. 159.

[35] *Taylor* v. *Twinberrow* [1930] 2 K.B. 16.

[36] *Fairweather* v. *St. Marylebone Property Co.* [1963] A.C. 510.

before the expiration of 12 years from the date when the second squatter took possession.

If a squatter abandons possession, and after an interval a second squatter takes possession, the second squatter has no right to add to his own period of possession that of the first squatter.[37]

---

[37] Limitation Act 1939, s. 10.

Chapter 22

REGISTRATION

(A) The Central Land Charges Register

PROVISION is made by the Land Charges Act 1972 [1] for the registration of certain rights against land [2] in five registers kept by the Land Registry in London.

(1) Pending actions, *i.e.* any pending legal proceeding affecting land, including bankruptcy petitions.

(2) Annuities, *i.e.* certain annuities affecting land created before 1926.

(3) Writs and order affecting land (excluding writs used to commence an action), *e.g.* writs of execution employed to enforce a judgment and bankruptcy receiving orders.

(4) Deeds of arrangement executed by debtors.

Registration in the registers mentioned above, other than that for annuities, is for a period of five years, but may be renewed.

(5) Land charges. There are six classes of these, of which mention will here be made only of classes C, D and F.

Class C

(i) *Puisne mortgage, i.e.* a legal mortgage not protected by deposit of title deeds with the mortgagee.

(ii) *Limited owner's charge, i.e.* a charge given by statute to a tenant for life or statutory owner who discharges estate duty or certain other liabilities.

(iii) *General equitable charge, i.e.* any equitable charge which is not registrable in any other class, is not protected by deposit of title deeds, and does not arise under a trust for sale or strict settlement or affect an interest under such a trust for sale or strict settlement. A common illustration is an equitable mortgage of a legal estate in land which is not protected by deposit of title deeds. It must be particularly noticed, on the other hand, that a mortgage or other charge of an equitable (beneficial) interest under a trust for sale or settlement is not registrable under the Act.

---

[1] This repealed and re-enacted most of the provisions of the Land Charges Act 1925.
[2] Other than registered land.

131

(iv) *Estate contract, i.e.* a contract to convey or create a legal estate made by a person who at the date of the contract owns a legal estate or is entitled to have such an estate conveyed to him: options to purchase and similar rights are included.

Class D

(i) *Death duties.* The revenue authorities have a charge on freeholds for estate duty payable thereon; the charge is registrable under this head, provided that the death occurred after 1925.

(ii) *Restrictive covenant.* A restrictive covenant affecting land is registrable if it was entered into after 1925 and is not a covenant in a lease.

(iii) *Equitable easement, i.e.* an equitable easement, profit or similar right created after 1925.

Class F

A charge affecting any land by virtue of the Matrimonial Homes Act 1967.[3]

Classes C, D and F

It will have been noticed that Class D land charges are registrable if created after 1925, and that a Class F land charge necessarily arises after 1967. A Class C land charge, however, is registrable irrespective of when it was created.

Registration and failure to register

In general registration of a registrable interest constitutes actual notice of the interest to all persons who acquire the land or any interest in it.[4] Failure to register the interest renders it void against a subsequent " purchaser," [5] and this is so even if that purchaser had actual notice of the interest [6] (although there are minor exceptions to this rule). But the definition of " purchaser " in the Land Charges Act differs with the type of land charge. Thus, for the purposes of Class C land charges (other than estate contracts entered into after 1925) and Class F land charges, " purchaser " means purchaser for value of any interest in the land, whether legal or equitable. For the purposes of Class D land charges, and estate contracts entered into after 1925, " purchaser " means purchaser of a legal estate for money or money's worth (which does not include marriage consideration). In either case a mortgagee or lessee is a " purchaser " for this purpose; but, if the narrower definition applies, only if he obtains a legal estate.

---

[3] See p. 97, *ante.*
[4] Law of Property Act 1925, s. 198.
[5] Land Charges Act 1972, s. 4.
[6] *Ibid.* s. 199.

System of registration

Registration of a registrable interest is against the name of the estate owner of the land affected, and not against the land itself. This is a serious defect in the system; it is not possible to ascertain what interests have been registered in respect of a particular plot of land since 1925 (when interests such as restrictive covenants and equitable easements created after 1925 became registrable) unless the names of the estate owners for that period are known. Although the deeds produced by a vendor to a purchaser as proof of title should reveal charges created during the period for which the title is adduced, and might also refer to earlier charges, there is a very real risk that both vendor and purchaser might be unaware of certain registered charges affecting the title. To meet this difficulty, section 25 of the Law of Property Act 1969 provides for the payment of compensation where a purchaser of any estate or interest has suffered loss by reason that the estate or interest is affected by a land charge [7] of which he had no knowledge, and which was registered against the name of any estate owner who was not a party to any transaction, or concerned in any event, comprised in the title which the purchaser was entitled to require. Compensation is payable to the purchaser by the Chief Land Registrar, and is recoverable by proceedings in the High Court.

Searches

Personal search may be made of the registers, but in practice official certificates of search are generally obtained by or on behalf of prospective purchasers. These are certificates of search made by responsible officials of the registry. Such a certificate is conclusive in favour of a purchaser. Moreover, if the purchaser completes his transaction before the expiration of 15 working days after the date of the certificate, he will not be affected by any entry in the register which is made after the date of the certificate, unless it is made in pursuance of a priority notice which had already been entered on the register before the certificate was issued.[8]

Priority notices

One who intends to take a registrable interest, e.g. a registrable mortgage, may lodge a priority notice on the register not less than 15 working days before the date of creation of the registrable interest. If he then registers his charge within 30 working days of the entry of the priority notice, the registration will date from the time when the interest was created.[8]

---

[7] Other than a local land charge.
[8] Land Charges Act 1972, s. 11.

(B) Local Land Charges

The Land Charges Act 1925, s. 15,[9] makes provision for the registration of certain interests in registers kept by local authorities, *i.e.* county councils and district or borough councils. A common example is road charges, *i.e.* charges against land which the local authority has in respect of the cost of making up a road adjoining that land. Registration is against the land itself. Failure to register the charge renders it void against a purchaser of a legal estate in the land for money or money's worth.

Provision is also made by certain other statutes for registration of various restrictions and other matters as if they were local land charges.[10] Although registrable in the local land charges registers, they are not, it seems, made local land charges for all purposes, and failure to register them would not necessarily render them void against a purchaser of the land.

(C) Registration of Title to Land

Quite different from the system of registration of charges referred to above is that of registration of title to land, which is now governed by the Land Registration Act 1925. This system is much more ambitious, and is designed to eliminate the investigation of title which normally takes place upon a purchase or mortgage of land. Registration of title to land is based upon the system of registration of title to shares. A shareholder in a company has issued to him a share certificate, which is prima facie evidence of his title to the shares. The company also maintains a register in which the names of the shareholders and the amounts of their holdings are entered. When a shareholder sells his shares he hands the share certificate to the purchaser together with a simple form of transfer signed by him; these documents are then lodged with the company, which alters its register and issues a new share certificate to the purchaser.

In the system of registration of title to land the share register kept by the company is replaced by a register of land holdings maintained by the state, and a land certificate takes the place of the share certificate. The general idea is that upon a transfer of the land the registered proprietor hands over the land certificate together with a simple deed of transfer executed by him to the purchaser, who then registers these documents with the registrar, whereupon the land register and the land certificate are amended, and the latter returned

---

[9] This section (which is not repealed by the Land Charges Act 1972) applies to both unregistered and registered land.
[10] Examples are an order under the New Towns Act 1946, a light obstruction notice under the Rights of Light Act 1959: see p. 91, *ante.*

to the transferee. Moreover, with some qualifications and exceptions, the state guarantees the accuracy of the register; if an error appears, the register may be rectified and an indemnity may be paid to any person suffering loss.

Compulsory registration

In certain areas, including the Greater London area and many boroughs and urban districts throughout the country, registration of title is compulsory.[11] When an area is declared a compulsory area the title to the fee simple must be registered upon the occasion of the first conveyance on sale thereafter, and the title to a leasehold must be registered when a lease for 40 years or more is granted or an existing lease having at least 40 years to run is assigned on sale. If application for registration is not made within two months of such a transaction, the transaction becomes void as to the legal estate.

Registrable interests

The only interests in respect of which title may be registered are the legal estates in land, *i.e.* the fee simple absolute in possession and the term of years absolute.[12] Title to a lease, however, may not be registered if the lease was granted for a term of 21 years or less or it contains an absolute prohibition against assignment or it is a mortgage term with a subsisting right of redemption.

Dispositions of registered land

Once the title to any land has been registered, any " disposition " of the land must itself be registered, otherwise it will be ineffective to dispose of a legal estate, and will create a minor interest only.[13] Thus, the grant of a lease of registered land must itself be registered if the lease is for more than 21 years.

Rights against registered land

Rights against land the title to which has been registered fall into three classes, namely registered interests, overriding interests and minor interests.

Registered interests

These are the legal estates the title to which has been registered under the Act.

---

[11] The compulsory areas as at April 1, 1974, are designated in the Registration of Title Order 1974. In other areas registration is voluntary, but voluntary registration is now restricted to certain cases specified by the registrar. (Land Registration Act 1966.)

[12] Title to a legal interest such as a rentcharge (either perpetual or for a term of years) may also be registered.

[13] See below.

Nature of title

Upon application for registration of the title to a *freehold*, the registrar may grant any one of three titles, *viz*. absolute, qualified and possessory. If an absolute title is granted, the title of the proprietor to the fee simple is guaranteed, subject only to interests entered on the register, to overriding interests (unless the register states that there are no such interests affecting the land), and minor interests of which the proprietor has notice. Registration with qualified title has the same effect, subject to some possible adverse interest which is *specified* in the register. Registration with possessory title has the same effect, except that no guarantee at all is given as to the absence of adverse interests subsisting at the date of first registration. Possessory title, therefore improves with the years, and indeed at the end of 15 years the registrar is bound to convert the title to absolute title, provided only that he is satisfied that the proprietor is in possession of the land.

Leasehold titles may be absolute, qualified, possessory or good leasehold. Absolute, qualified and possessory titles have the same effect as the corresponding freehold titles, except that the registered proprietor is, of course, subject to all the obligations of the lease. Absolute leasehold title guarantees the title of the landlord to grant the lease as well as the title of the leasehold proprietor to the lease itself. When good leasehold title is granted no guarantee is given with regard to the landlord's right to grant the lease, but in other respects the title is the same as absolute title. The registrar is bound to convert possessory leasehold title to good leasehold title after 10 years, if he is satisfied that the proprietor is in possession of the land.

Conversion of title

In addition to the rules given above, the registrar upon a transfer for value may convert qualified or possessory title to absolute or good leasehold title, and may convert good leasehold title to absolute title. Further, after 10 years the registrar may convert good leasehold into absolute title, if satisfied that the lessees have been in possession during that period.

Overriding interests

These are interests which will bind a purchaser of the land whether or not they are noted on the register, and whether or not he has notice of their existence. All registered land is deemed to be subject to any overriding interests subsisting in reference thereto and falling within the categories listed in section 70 of the Land Registration Act 1925.

The most important overriding interests are set out in the following paragraphs of that section:

(a) Easements, profits, public rights, etc.

(f) Rights acquired or in the course of being acquired under the Limitation Acts.

(g) The rights of every person in actual occupation of the land or in receipt of the rents and profits thereof, save where inquiry is made of such person and the rights are not disclosed.

(k) Leases for a term not exceeding twenty-one years granted at a rent without taking a fine.

Paragraph (g) calls for further comment. The rights to which it refers are confined to those of a proprietary character, and do not include personal rights, such as those created by a mere licence, which are not binding on third parties.[14] Rights arising under a contract of sale, or an agreement for a lease, or an option, are included,[15] with the result that whereas in the case of unregistered land such rights would not bind the land unless they were registered under the Land Charges Act 1972, they will be binding as overriding interests if the title to the land is registered—provided that the person asserting them is in actual occupation.[16] The rights of a beneficiary under a trust may also constitute an overriding interest under this paragraph,[17] notwithstanding that the Act expressly provides [18] that persons dealing with a registered estate shall not be affected with notice of a trust express, implied or constructive.

Minor interests

These comprise all interests in registered land other than registered interests and overriding interests. They fall into two classes:

(a) Interests, such as those of beneficiaries under a settlement or trust for sale, which (as in the case of unregistered land) are capable of being overreached, and which when overreached do not bind a purchaser even if they have been protected by some kind of entry on the register.

---

[14] *Strand Securities Ltd.* v. *Caswell* [1965] Ch. 958, C.A.; *National Provincial Bank Ltd.* v. *Ainsworth* [1965] A.C. 1175.

[15] *Bridges* v. *Mees* [1957] Ch. 475; *Woolwich Equitable B.S.* v. *Marshall* [1952] Ch. 1; *Webb* v. *Pollmount Ltd.* [1966] Ch. 584.

[16] If he is not in actual occupation, they will constitute minor interests only, and as such require protection by notice or caution.

[17] *Hodgson* v. *Marks* [1971] Ch. 918, C.A.; as to unregistered land, *cf.* *Caunce* v. *Caunce* [1969] 1 W.L.R. 286.

[18] s. 74. With respect to beneficial interests under a strict settlement, however, s. 86 (2) provides that these shall take effect as minor interests and not otherwise.

(b) Interests, such as estate contracts and restrictive covenants, which will bind a purchaser if they have been protected by an appropriate entry on the register, but not otherwise.

Minor interests may be protected by the entry of restrictions, or notice, or caution, or inhibition, on the register.

Restrictions are appropriate to protect any minor interest of class (a) above. They are entered at the request of the registered proprietor and indicate, *e.g.* that capital money is to be paid to the trustees of the settlement or trust for sale.

Notice is the primary method of protecting interests which are not capable of being overreached (class (b) above) and which, in the case of unregistered land, would be registrable under the Land Charges Act 1972.

Caution. Any person interested in registered land may lodge a caution against dealings with the land. This entitles the cautioner to be notified by the registrar of proposed dealings with the land, and to object within a specified period. A caution is frequently lodged as a means of protecting a minor interest, such as that of a purchaser under an estate contract,[19] where the cautioner is unable to register a notice because the registered proprietor has not furnished his land certificate.[20]

Inhibition. This is entered in pursuance of an order of the court or of the registrar in circumstances such as the bankruptcy of the registered proprietor. Its effect generally is to prevent dealings with the land until further order.

Mortgages

Mortgages of registered land may be effected in three ways:

(i) *Registered charge.* The charge must be made by deed and the land certificate must be deposited in the registry. A certificate of charge is then issued to the mortgagee. The charge is entered in the charges register, and the priority of successive registered charges generally follows the order of entry.

(ii) *Unregistered mortgage,* protected by entry of a mortgage caution in the proprietorship register.

(iii) *Deposit of land certificate with the mortgagee,* protected by entry of a notice in the charges register.[21]

---

[19] It may also be used to protect the interest of a person beneficially entitled under a trust for sale (*Elias* v. *Mitchell* [1972] Ch. 652).
[20] Notices must be entered on the charges register (see below) and accordingly on the land certificate.
[21] As to the efficacy of this method, see *Barclay's Bank Ltd.* v. *Taylor* [1973] Ch. 63, C.A.

The register

This is divided into three parts:

(i) *The property register,* which describes the land and the estate (*e.g.* the fee simple) the title to which is registered, and any interests, such as easements, which are known to be appurtenant to the land.

(ii) *The proprietorship register,* which states the kind of title (*e.g.* absolute) which has been granted and the name and address of the proprietor; it also contains a note of any cautions, inhibitions or restrictions which have been entered.

(iii) *The charges register,* which consists of entries of mortgages and other interests adverse to the land; notices are entered in this part of the register.

The system of registration of charges in the central land charges register does not apply to registered land; but registration of local land charges takes place in the same way as if the title to the land were not registered.

Index of minor interests

As we have seen,[22] under the rule in *Dearle* v. *Hall* when successive assignments or charges of an equitable interest in property take place the priority of those dealings, in general, follows the order in which written notice of them is given to the trustees of the settlement or trust. When, however, the assignment or charge is of an equitable interest in land the title to which is registered, the assignee or mortgagee, instead of giving notice to the trustees, should enter a priority inhibition or priority caution in the Index of Minor Interests, which is maintained for that purpose. A priority inhibition is used for an absolute assignment, and a priority caution for a mortgage or charge. Priority follows the order of entry of these inhibitions or cautions.[23] It will be noticed that the title Index of Minor Interests is most misleading, because it is not in any sense an index of minor interests.

---

[22] See p. 117, *ante.*
[23] Land Registration Act 1925, s. 102. Land Registration Rules 1925, rr. 11, 29.

CHAPTER 23

DEVOLUTION ON DEATH

WHEN a person dies his property devolves on (*i.e.* passes by operation of law to) his personal representatives. These personal representatives may be executors or administrators. An executor is a person appointed by the will of the deceased to execute the terms of the will. An administrator is a person appointed by the court to administer the deceased's estate when he has died intestate or when he has died testate but without leaving an executor who is able and willing to act. An executor who is willing to act must obtain a grant of probate from the court and is then said to prove the testator's will; but the will, not the probate, is the source of his authority, and he becomes executor immediately upon the death of the deceased. An administrator is appointed by the grant of letters of administration by the court and he owes his position entirely to this grant.

There are a very few exceptions to the rule that a deceased person's property devolves upon his personal representatives. Amongst these i an entailed interest which a deceased person has not barred during his life-time or by his will: this passes directly to the heir.[1]

The duties of personal representatives are:

(i) to collect the assets belonging to the estate,

(ii) to pay the funeral, testamentary and administration expense and the deceased's debts, and

(iii) to distribute any surplus amongst the persons entitled under the deceased's will or the law of intestacy.

Testamentary liberty

Many systems of law, and in particular those, such as the Scots law which are derived from the Roman Law, do not allow complete testamentary liberty: a man may dispose of only part of his estate by his will, and the rest goes to certain relatives prescribed by law English law has never adopted this position and in general it ha allowed complete testamentary liberty, although originally the law c curtesy and of dower made some provision for a surviving husban or wife.

Curtesy was a life estate in his wife's lands which the law on certai conditions gave to a surviving husband. The wife had to be seised c the land for an estate of inheritance and it was necessary that issu of the marriage capable of inheriting the land should have been bor

---

[1] See p. 155, *post.*

alive. In the period immediately before 1926 the husband had no claim to curtesy if his wife had disposed of the land *inter vivos* or by her will. Curtesy still applies after 1925 when a wife is a tenant in tail in possession at her death and she has not barred the entail by her will.

On much the same conditions the law gave to a surviving wife a life estate in one-third of her husband's lands, and this was known as her dower. In this case the birth of issue capable of inheriting was not required, but it must have been possible for such issue to be born; *e.g.* if land had been granted to A and the heirs of his body by his wife Mary, a wife other than Mary could not claim dower out of the land in question. The widow's dower might be assigned to her by metes and bounds, *i.e.* one-third of the land might be allocated to her for her life. Alternatively, by agreement with the heir or other person entitled to the land she might be given the right to receive one-third of the rents and profits of the land. After the Dower Act 1833, a wife could not claim dower if the husband had disposed of the land *inter vivos* or by his will, or if he had made a declaration by deed or by will barring the wife's right to dower. A claim to dower cannot arise on a death after 1925.[2]

The Inheritance (Family Provision) Act 1938

This Act[3] in effect places some restriction upon that testamentary liberty which was previously allowed. A dependant may apply to the court for the payment of maintenance[4] out of the income of the deceased's estate on the ground that reasonable provision is not made for him or her by the will or by the operation of the law of intestacy or (in cases of partial intestacy) both. For the purposes of the Act a dependant is a surviving husband or wife, a son who has not attained the age of 21 years, a daughter who has not married, or a son or a daughter who is incapable of supporting himself or herself through some mental or physical defect. Adopted children are included.[5] In considering the application the court must take into account all relevant circumstances, including the dependant's conduct towards the deceased and the deceased's reasons for not having made provision or further provision for the dependant, if these can be ascertained; any statement in writing signed by the deceased and dated in which he states his

[2] There is one exception of a transitional character relating to a person who is of full age and of unsound mind at the end of 1925.
[3] As amended by the Intestates' Estates Act 1952, the Family Provision Act 1966 and the Family Law Reform Act 1969.
[4] The court has power to order payment of a lump sum in lieu of maintenance:
[5] As also are illegitimate children of a person dying after December 31, 1969 (Family Law Reform Act 1969, s. 18).

reasons is admissible in evidence for this purpose. Nevertheless, the test of whether reasonable provision has in fact been made is objective; " The question is not whether the testator acted reasonably, but whether the will makes reasonable provision for the applicant." [6]

Maintenance payable to a husband or wife will cease on re-marriage; to a son on his attaining the age of 21 years; to a son who is under disability on the cessation of his disability; to a daughter who has not married or is under disability, on marriage or the cessation of the disability, whichever is the later. In any event maintenance ceases on death.

The Matrimonial Causes Act 1965, s. 26, gives a somewhat similar right to an ex-husband or ex-wife of the deceased where the marriage has been annulled by a decree of nullity or dissolved by a decree of divorce.

When maintenance has been ordered under these provisions the terms of the will operate only so far as they are consistent with the duty of the personal representatives to pay the maintenance ordered.

---

[6] *Per* Lord Denning M.R., in *Millward* v. *Shenton* [1972] 1 W.L.R. 711, at p. 715.

CHAPTER 24

WILLS

IN general, if a will is to be valid the testator must be of full age and otherwise of sound testamentary capacity and the will must be executed with the formalities prescribed by section 9 of the Wills Act 1837.

Formalities

By section 9, (a) the will must be in writing; (b) it must be signed by the testator or by someone else for him in his presence and at his direction; (c) the signature must be at the foot or end of the will; (d) the testator must make or acknowledge his signature in the presence of two witnesses present at the same time and (e) the witnesses must then attest the will in the presence of the testator (but not necessarily in the presence of each other). An attestation clause, *i.e.* a clause by which the witnesses certify that the will has been signed in their presence and that they have signed in the presence of the testator, is commonly included. Such a clause is not legally necessary, but it greatly facilitates proof of the will after the testator's death.

One or two points on section 9 may be noticed here.

Any mark made by the testator counts as his signature for this purpose if it was designed to fulfil the function of a signature, *i.e.* to authenticate the document.

The provision that the signature must be at the foot or end of the will was greatly modified by the Wills Act Amendment Act 1852, which provides in effect that the signature shall be deemed to be at the foot or end, wherever it is in fact, if it is evident from the document that the signature was intended to authenticate the will; but nothing which was inserted after the will was signed, or which follows the signature in space, will form part of the will. Thus in one case the will was written on several sheets and the signatures of the testator and witnesses were on the top sheet, which was otherwise blank. It was held that the whole will was validly executed, as it was evident from the document that the signatures were intended to be read last.[1] Where (as in this illustration) the will is on several sheets only one of which is signed, those sheets must be fastened together at the time of execution; but it is sufficient for this purpose that they are held together by the pressure of the testator's thumb.[1]

The " presence " referred to in the section is physical presence and mental presence. Physical presence means the ability to see what is

---

[1] *In the Estate of Little* [1960] 1 W.L.R. 495. Contrast *Re Beadle* [1974] 1 W.L.R. 417.

143

being done if one chooses to look (or that one would have had that ability if one had had the gift of sight). Mental presence means the mental capacity to understand the character of the act. Thus, although an infant can be a good witness, it is essential that he should be old enough to understand the character of the act of witnessing. It may be mentioned that (generally, at any rate) a blind man cannot be a witness, because the nature of his disability is inconsistent with the act of witnessing.[2]

There is no provision for a witness to acknowledge his signature. It is, therefore, necessary that both the witnesses should sign the will after the testator has either signed the will in the presence of the witnesses or acknowledged his signature in their presence.[3]

Privileged testators

Certain privileged testators may make valid wills although they are under full age and without complying with the formalities prescribed by section 9.[4] Such a will may even be made by word of mouth, in which case it is called a nuncupative will. A privileged testator is one who at the time of making the will is in one of the following categories:

(i) A soldier in actual military service.
(ii) A mariner or seaman at sea.
(iii) A member of the Royal Navy or Royal Marines so situated that had he been a soldier he would have been in actual military service.

" Soldier " includes members of the Royal Air Force and women members of the Army and R.A.F. The words " in actual military service " mean that the soldier must be serving *in connection with* hostilities, whether those hostilities have broken out, or are apprehended, or have concluded. Thus a soldier is in actual military service as soon as he receives mobilisation orders even if he has not yet joined his unit, and a member of an army of occupation is in such service even though hostilities have long since concluded.

The words " at sea " in the expression " mariner or seaman at sea " refer to the status of the mariner or seaman: they do not require that he should in fact be at sea at the time of making the will. Thus a member of the crew of a ship is " at sea " while he is on shore leave.

Members of the Royal Navy are included with merchant seamen in the second category mentioned above; the third category is limited to them and members of the Royal Marines. One effect of the third

[2] *In the Estate of Gibson* [1949] P. 434.
[3] See *Wyatt* v. *Berry* [1893] P. 5; *Re Groffman* [1969] 1 W.L.R. 733.
[4] Wills Act 1837, s. 11, as amended by the Wills (Soldiers and Sailors) Act 1918.

category is to make a member of the Royal Navy or Royal Marines a privileged testator from the moment that he receives mobilisation orders in connection with hostilities, even if he has not yet joined his ship; as we have seen, a soldier is in actual military service as soon as he receives mobilisation orders.

A will made by a privileged testator remains valid indefinitely [5]; e.g. the validity of a soldier's will is not limited to the duration of his military service.

Revocation

A will may be revoked in three ways, viz. by a later will or codicil, by marriage and by destruction.

(a) Later will

A later will (or codicil) revokes an earlier will if it shows an intention to that effect. Such an intention is clearly shown if the later will contains a clause expressly revoking all earlier wills.[6] The formal phrase " This is the last will and testament of me " does not of itself show an intention to revoke earlier wills.[7] If a later will does not show an intention to revoke an earlier will in its entirety, the two documents will be read together and the earlier will be revoked only so far as it is inconsistent with the later. For example, if the same property is specifically devised to different persons in the two wills, but the devise in the second will is contingent upon the devisee attaining a certain age, the devisee under the earlier will will be entitled to the property unless and until the contingency is fulfilled.[8]

(b) Marriage

Marriage revokes any will made before that marriage.[9] There are two exceptions to this rule:

(i) That part of the will which makes an appointment under a power of appointment possessed by the testator will not be revoked by the marriage (although all the rest of the will will be revoked), unless the instrument creating the power of appointment provides that in default of appointment the property shall go to the executor, administrator, heir, or statutory next of kin of the person to whom the power is given (i.e. the testator).[10] The instrument creating a

---

[5] Unless and until he revokes it.
[6] But a revocation clause in a standard printed form of will may be disregarded if the court is satisfied that the testator did not in fact intend to revoke other wills (Re Phelan, decd. [1972] Fam. 33).
[7] Simpson v. Foxon [1907] P. 54.
[8] Duffield v. Duffield (1829) 1 D. & C. 268.
[9] Wills Act 1837, s. 18.
[10] Ibid.

power of appointment normally provides who shall be entitled to the property if the donee of the power dies without making an appointment, *i.e.* without making an effective appointment; this provision is known as a gift over in default of appointment. If this gift over provides that in default of appointment the property shall go to the executor, administrator, etc. of the donee of the power, then any appointment made by the will of the donee of the power will be revoked by his subsequent marriage. But if the gift over provides that the property shall go to anyone else, then an appointment made by the will of the donee of the power will not be revoked by his subsequent marriage.

(ii) A will made after 1925 and expressed to be made in contemplation of a marriage will not be revoked by that marriage.[11]

(c) *Destruction*

A will is revoked by burning, tearing or otherwise destroying the same if the destruction is done by the testator, or by some other person in his presence and at his direction, with the intention of revoking the will.[12] Thus, there must be both the fact of destruction (not, *e.g.* merely writing " these are revoked " across the document)[13] and the intention to revoke. Destruction of that part of the will which contains the signatures is sufficient.

If a testator keeps his will in his own possession and at his death the will cannot be found, the presumption is that he has destroyed the will with the intention of revoking it, but this presumption is rebuttable by evidence to the contrary.[14]

Revival

Revival means restoring a revoked will to life without the necessity of executing a new will in the same terms.

A will that has been revoked by destruction cannot be revived. A will that has been revoked by another will or by marriage can be revived either by re-execution of the document or by the execution of a further will or codicil showing an intention to revive the revoked will; but a revoked will cannot be revived in any other way, and, in particular, if will no. 1 has been revoked by will no. 2 the revocation of will no. 2 will not of itself revive will no. 1.[15]

Conditional revocation

The revocation of a will may be conditional, in which case it will

---

[11] Law of Property Act 1925, s. 177.
[12] Wills Act 1837, s. 20.
[13] *Cheese* v. *Lovejoy* (1877) 2 P.D. 251.
[14] *Sugden* v. *Lord St. Leonards* (1876) 1 P.D. 154.
[15] Wills Act 1837, s. 22.

not take effect unless the condition is fulfilled. The doctrine of dependent relative revocation is a particular application of this principle: if a will (or part of it) is revoked for the purpose only of substituting some other will for it, and that other will is not in fact brought into existence, the revocation does not become effective. An obvious illustration is when a testator who has given instructions for the preparation of a new will destroys an existing will, but dies before he is able to execute the new document; the inference in such a case will generally be that he destroyed the old will for the purpose only of substituting the new will, in which case the destruction will not revoke the old will. Again, if will no. 1 is revoked by will no. 2, and the testator destroys will no. 2 in the mistaken [16] belief that he will thereby revive will no. 1, will no. 2 will not be revoked. A further illustration will appear under the next heading.

Alterations

An alteration made in the document before its execution is part of the will. However, as there is a presumption that an alteration was made after execution, it is desirable (although not legally necessary) that any such alteration should be initialled by the testator and witnesses; otherwise when the time comes to prove the will it may be impossible to rebut the presumption.

An alteration made by the testator after the execution of the will is not generally part of the will, unless the alteration has itself been executed as a will, for which purpose intialling by the testator and witnesses is sufficient. There is, however, an exception where a testator *obliterates* words so effectively that the original wording is no longer " apparent," because in this case probate will be granted of the will with a blank for the obliterated words, so that the alteration will be effective even if it has not been executed as a will.[17] The original wording is not " apparent " unless it is visible to the eye, with or without the aid of a magnifying glass, strong light or the like. The court will not tamper with the document in an endeavour to read the original words, *e.g.* by removing a piece of paper which has been pasted over certain words. Moreover, extrinsic evidence is not in general admissible to prove the original wording, and for this reason an infra-red photograph of the document (which might reveal the original wording) cannot be given in evidence. When, however, a testator obliterates words and *substitutes* others in the mistaken belief that the substituted words will be effective, the doctrine of dependent relative revocation applies and extrinsic evidence, including an infra-red photograph,[18] is admissible to prove the original wording.

---

[16] *Supra.*   [17] Wills Act 1837, s. 21.
[18] *In the Goods of Itter* [1950] P. 130.

It may be mentioned here that when a will has been mutilated or destroyed without the testator's authority, or has been accidentally destroyed or lost, extrinsic evidence is always admissible to prove the contents of the will; for example the will may be proved by means of a copy or the oral testimony of one who can swear to the contents of the document.[19]

Gifts to witnesses and their spouses

Section 15 of the Wills Act 1837 provides that any gift by will to a person who attests the will as a witness, or to the husband or wife of such a witness, shall be void. The spouse of a witness does not fall within this rule unless he or she was married to the witness at the date of the execution of the will, and the rule is excluded if the will is confirmed by a codicil which is not attested by the beneficiary or his or her spouse. By the Wills Act 1968, the attestation of a will by a beneficiary or the spouse of a beneficiary shall be disregarded if the will is duly executed without his attestation and without that of any other such person.

Section 15 has been applied to a charging clause in a will allowing the trustee of the will to charge for his services as trustee; such a trustee cannot charge for his services if he or his spouse has attested the will.[20] On the other hand, the rule has been held inapplicable to a witness who was appointed trustee after the testator's death; he was therefore held entitled to charge for his services under a charging clause in the will.[21]

Criminal homicide

A person who criminally causes the death of another forfeits any benefit that he would have taken under that person's will or intestacy.[22]

Lapse

In general, if the will confers a benefit upon a person who predeceases the testator, the gift lapses and fails. Usually when a gift lapses the property falls into the residuary estate, but if the gift itself is of the residuary estate, or of a share of the residue, the property passes to the testator's statutory next of kin: there is an intestacy with regard to that property. The doctrine of lapse has no application when property is given to two or more persons jointly and one of them predeceases the testator; the survivor or survivors then take the whole of the property.

---

[19] *Sugden* v. *Lord St. Leonards* (1876) 1 P.D. 154.
[20] *Re Pooley* (1888) 40 Ch.D. 1.
[21] *Re Royce's Will Trusts* [1959] Ch. 626.
[22] For a recent example, see *Re Giles, decd.* [1972] Ch. 544.

There are the following exceptions to the doctrine of lapse:

(i) When the gift is made in discharge of a moral obligation (*e.g.* when a woman who has promised to pay her son's debts leaves a legacy to one of the son's creditors) [23] then if the donee predeceases the testator the gift can be claimed by the donee's personal representatives on behalf of his estate.

(ii) By section 32 of the Wills Act 1837, if property is left by will to any person in tail and the donee predeceases the testator, leaving issue living at the testator's death who are capable of inheriting under the entail, there is no lapse and the property goes as if the donee had survived the testator and died immediately afterwards. The result is that the property passes to the donee's heir in tail.

(iii) By section 33 of the same Act, if property is given by will to a child or remoter issue of the testator for any interest which is not to cease with the death of the donee, and the donee predeceases the testator leaving issue living at the testator's death, there is no lapse and the property goes as if the donee had survived the testator and died immediately afterwards. The result, in general, is that the property can be claimed by the donee's personal representatives on behalf of his estate. It then goes to the persons who are entitled under the terms of the donee's will or the law of intestacy as if it had formed part of the donee's estate *at the date of his death*.[24] Thus, if T leaves property to C (a child of T), who predeceases T but leaves issue who survive T, and C by his will has left all his property to X, and X survives C, then upon the death of T the property given by T's will to C can be claimed by C's personal representatives on behalf of C's estate. It will then pass under C's will to X, or, if X has died before T,[24] to X's personal representatives.

It has been held that section 33 does not apply to an appointment made under a special power of appointment possessed by the testator.[25] Nor does it normally apply to class gifts, *e.g.* a gift to " all my children," because such a gift is prima facie construed to refer to the members of the class who are living at the date of the testator's death.[26]

Commorientes

If there is no evidence as to which of two persons survived the other, then for the purposes of succession to property the presumption is that the younger survived the elder.[27] There is an exception to this rule in the law of intestacy which we shall notice later.[28]

---

[23] *Re Leach* [1948] Ch. 232.
[24] *Re Basioli* [1953] Ch. 367.
[25] *Holyland* v. *Lewin* (1883) 26 Ch.D. 266.
[26] *Olney* v. *Bates* (1855) 3 Drew. 319.
[27] Law of Property Act 1925, s. 184.
[28] See p. 159, *post*.

The will and its construction

It must be conclusively presumed that the deceased's testamentary wishes are those which he has set out in the written will (we are not here concerned with nuncupative wills). Extrinsic evidence is not admissible to add to, vary or contradict the written instrument, although such evidence may sometimes be admitted in order to establish what the will of the deceased is.

Once it has been determined that a written instrument is to be regarded as the last will and testament of the deceased, the question of construction arises, *i.e.* it becomes necessary to determine the *meaning* of the instrument. The primary rule here is that the words must be given their ordinary grammatical meaning. But this rule may be departed from in certain circumstances, *e.g.* where the ordinary meaning of the words would give rise to an absurdity. In general, the same canons of construction apply to a will as apply to any other written instrument, and the topic is not one that can be considered at length here. We must, however, consider briefly the question how far extrinsic evidence is admissible to assist the court in its task of construction. The general rule is that such evidence is not admissible, but there are two main exceptions to this rule:

(a) Under what is sometimes called the *armchair principle*, evidence is always admissible as to what the facts were at the date when the testator executed the will, in order that the court may be able, as it were, to seat itself in the testator's armchair and look at the will through his eyes. Extrinsic evidence is accordingly admissible to show the meaning of terms which had a special meaning for the testator by reason of the locality in which he lived or the trade at which he worked or by reason of family usage. For example, in one case,[29] where the testator left everything to " mother," evidence was admitted to show that in the testator's family he referred to his wife as " mother."

(b) Extrinsic evidence is admissible to resolve an *equivocation*, *i.e.* a difficulty which arises when an attempt is made to put into operation the provisions of the will because it is found that there are two or more persons or things which equally well answer some term of the will. But extrinsic evidence is not admissible to *create* an ambiguity which does not exist if the words are given their normal meaning. For example, if a testator makes a gift by will to " my niece," and he has only one legitimate niece there is no ambiguity, because the reference must be taken as being to the legitimate niece[30]; extrinsic evidence is not therefore admissible to show that the testator intended

---

[29] *Thorn* v. *Dickens* [1906] W.N. 54.
[30] This presumption no longer applies in relation to dispositions made after December 31, 1969 (Family Law Reform Act 1969, s. 15).

to benefit an illegitimate niece—to admit the evidence would be to
admit it in order to create an ambiguity.[31] But if the gift is to "my
nephew" and the testator has two nephews, both by legitimate
relationship, extrinsic evidence is admissible to show which of those
two nephews he intended to benefit; there is a genuine equivocation.
In such a case if the evidence, when admitted, shows that the testator
intended to benefit a third, and illegitimate, nephew, that illegitimate
nephew will take; once the evidence has been admitted, the full
consequences of its admission must be accepted.[32]

Extrinsic evidence is not admissible to resolve a *contradiction*; if a
contradiction cannot be resolved by reference to the instrument as a
whole, the later provision in the will will prevail over the earlier.

The following additional rules may also be noticed:

(i) *A will speaks from the death*

A will speaks from the death with regard to the property disposed
of by it, *i.e.* it is to be construed as if it had been executed at the
moment of death, unless a contrary intention appears.[33] For example,
a gift of "all my realty" prima facie means all the realty that the
testator has at the date of his death. But the court may find evidence
of a contrary intention when there is a specific gift of property which
is not liable to increase or decrease (*e.g.* "my piano"); in such cases
the reference is generally taken to be to the property described which
the testator possessed at the date of making the will. The gift is then
said to be adeemed, and it fails, if the testator afterwards disposes
of that property; for example, if the gift is of "my piano" and the
testator after executing the will disposes of that piano, the legatee will
get nothing [34]—he will not get another piano which the testator pur-
chases in substitution, unless after that purchase the will containing
the specific bequest is confirmed by codicil.[35]

(ii) *The class closing rules*

When a will contains a gift to a class of persons there are somewhat
elaborate rules for deciding what members of the class are intended
to be benefited. For example, if the will gives property to "John's
children," does the testator intend that the property should go to all
John's children, whether born at the date of the testator's death or
to be born thereafter, or is the reference only to such of John's children

[31] *Re Fish* [1894] 2 Ch. 83.
[32] *Re Jackson* [1933] Ch. 237.
[33] Wills Act 1837, s. 24.
[34] *Re Sikes* [1927] 1 Ch. 364.
[35] *Re Reeves* [1928] Ch. 351 (gift of "all my interest in my present lease"
of certain property held to cover a new lease of the property, the will having
been confirmed by codicil after the grant of the new lease).

as are living at the testator's death? The prima facie rule for immediate class gifts is that if there is any member of the class in existence at the date of the testator's death the reference is to the members of the class who are living at the testator's death, but that if at that date there is no member of the class in existence after-born members of the class are intended to be benefited. This rule [36] sometimes prevents an infringement of the perpetuity rule which would otherwise occur; for example, if there is a gift to " John's grandchildren," and at the date of the testator's death John has a grandchild who is then living, the gift prima facie is taken to be to that grandchild only (or, if there are more than one then living, to those grandchildren only). But if at that date there is no grandchild living, the reference prima facie is to all John's grandchildren born at any time in the future, and the gift then infringes the perpetuity rule [37] unless John himself was dead at the date of the testator's death.

A similar rule applies to contingent gifts. For example, if there is a gift to John's children who attain 21, and at the date of the testator's death any child has attained 21, the gift prima facie is taken to be to such of John's children *living at the testator's death* who attain the age of 21. But if no child has then attained 21, the class remains open until some child attains 21, and the property then goes to all the children who are living *at that date* and who attain 21.

Other rules apply to gifts in remainder and to gifts of reversionary interests.

(iii) *Appointments under powers of appointment*

If a testator is the donee of a *general* power of appointment which he can exercise by his will, and he leaves a will which does not contain an express appointment under the power, but which contains a general devise or bequest, there is an implied appointment in favour of the general devisee or legatee.[38] For example, if the testator in his will says, " I leave all my property to A," not only will A take the testator's property, but also there will be an implied appointment in A's favour under the general power possessed by the testator, so that he will also be entitled to the property over which the testator had the power of appointment.

A general devise or bequest does not impliedly exercise a *special* power possessed by the testator.

---

[36] Commonly referred to as the rule in *Andrews* v. *Partington* (1791) 3 Bro.C.C. 401. The rule is subject to any contrary intention expressed in the will (see *Re Edmonson* [1971] 1 W.L.R. 1652).
[37] Subject to the provisions of the Perpetuities and Accumulations Act 1964 (see pp. 75, 76, *ante*).
[38] Wills Act 1837, s. 27.

(iv) *Gift " to A but if he dies without issue then over to B "*

Originally a gift in these or similar terms was construed as showing an intention to give a fee tail in the property to A. But this construction was abolished by section 29 of the Wills Act 1837, which provided, in effect, that under such a gift the property should go initially to A and that its final destination should be decided according to whether or not A had any issue living at the date of his death. If at his death A has issue then living the property forms part of his estate in fee simple or, if it is personalty, absolutely. But if at his death he has no issue living, the property goes over to B for a similar estate or interest. An exception to this rule was enacted by the Conveyancing Act 1882, with regard to land, and by section 134 of the Law of Property Act 1925, with regard to all property. Under this exception if at any time during A's lifetime any of his issue attain the age of 18,[39] the gift over to B at once fails, with the result that the property then belongs to A in fee simple or absolutely. This provision applies to deeds as well as to wills, and it applies whatever interest is granted to A unless it be an entailed interest. Thus section 134 applies if the property is given " to A for life," or " to A in fee simple," with a gift over to B if A dies without issue.[40]

(v) *The rule in Wild's Case*

Before 1926 if a testator left realty to A " and his children " a question of construction arose as to whether the testator intended the land to go in fee simple to A and his children jointly, or intended A to have a fee tail in the land. One might have thought that the first construction represented the obvious intention of the testator, but the view was taken that the words " and his children " might have been used as words of limitation, being intended to be synonymous with " and his issue " and therefore to give a fee tail to A.[41] The prima facie rule adopted by the court, and known as the rule in *Wild's Case*,[42] was that if when the testator made his will A had no children, the testator intended A to have a fee tail, but that if when the testator made the will A had a child or children, the testator intended the land to go in fee simple to A and his children jointly (A would then take the land jointly with such of his children as were living *at the testator's death*). On the death of a testator after 1925 the second branch of the rule is unaffected, but when the first branch would

---

[39] As substituted by the Family Law Reform Act 1969, s. 1, with effect from January 1, 1970.
[40] Land subject to such a limitation is settled land, and A is "tenant for life," until issue of A attains 18 or until A dies without issue. See p. 50, *ante.*
[41] See Chap. 4.
[42] (1599) 6 Co.Rep. 16b.

apply the effect today cannot be that A takes a fee tail—as we have seen a fee tail can be created today only by technical common law or statutory expressions, which do not include the words " and his children." It is uncertain what the effect is in such case, but it may be assumed that A takes the fee simple.[43]

---

[43] See Chap. 4.

CHAPTER 25

INTESTACY

Survivals of the Old Law

ON a death intestate before 1926 the deceased's realty went to his heir, ascertained by applying the old common law canons of descent, as somewhat amended by statute, whereas his personalty went to his statutory next of kin under the old Statutes of Distribution. When the death occurs after 1925 the general rule is that both realty and personalty are governed by the provisions of the Administration of Estates Act 1925.[1] As an exception, an unbarred entail still devolves upon the heir, ascertained by applying the old realty canons of descent. For this reason some knowledge of the old canons is still required by the lawyer today. Another reason is that the word " heir " or " heirs " may be used as a word of purchase in a post-1925 instrument,[2] in which case the reference must be taken to be to the heir as ascertained under the old canons of descent: there is no heir under the Administration of Estates Act 1925. An unbarred entail can, of course, devolve only upon an heir found amongst descendants of the original tenant in tail, and we will confine our attention to the rules applicable to finding an heir amongst descendants. These rules are as follows:

(i) Descent is traced from the last purchaser of the land, *i.e.* from the person who last acquired the land otherwise than by descent on intestacy. When considering the descent of an unbarred entail this rule presents no difficulty, because the last purchaser is always the original tenant in tail.

(ii) Males are preferred to females in the same degree.

(iii) An elder male is preferred to a younger male in the same degree.

(iv) Amongst·females there is no preference for an elder over a younger, and all females in the same degree take equally as coparceners.

(v) If a person would have been heir (including co-heir) but for the fact that he is dead, then if that person has left issue, those issue, or such of them as are preferred under the above rules, have the right to represent their deceased parent.

In the following examples M stands for male and F for female.

---

[1] As amended by the Intestates' Estates Act 1952, the Family Provision Act 1966 and the Family Law Reform Act 1969.
[2] See p. 8, *ante.*

Example 1

T, the original tenant in tail, has four children, M1, F1, M2, F2, born in that order, all of whom survive him. The males are preferred to the females, and the elder male to the younger male, so that M1 is the sole heir.

Example 2

The facts are the same, except that M1 has pre-deceased T, leaving two children, a son and a daughter, both of whom survive T. M1's son, being preferred to his sister, has the right to represent his deceased father and is therefore the sole heir. Had M1 left only a daughter, she would have had the right to represent her deceased father, and she therefore would have been the sole heir. It will be observed that in consequence of rule (v), the whole of the elder son's line is preferred to the younger son and his line.

Example 3

T, the original tenant in tail, has had two children, F1 and F2, both of whom survive him. The two daughters together constitute the heir, taking between themselves as co-parceners. There is no preference for an elder female over a younger female.

Example 4

The facts are the same as in Example 3, except that F1 has pre-deceased T, leaving two children, a son and a daughter, who survive T. F1's son, being preferred to his sister, has the exclusive right to represent his deceased mother. He, therefore, and F2 together constitute the heir.

Example 5

T, the original tenant in tail, has two sons, M1 and M2, both of whom survive him. M1 therefore becomes the sole heir and enjoys the land in tail. Later M1 dies, a bachelor, without having barred the entail. Upon the death of M1 the land devolves upon M2. This example shows how necessary it may be to remember the rule that descent is to be traced from the last purchaser, *i.e.* where the devolution of an unbarred entail is in point, the original tenant in tail.

It may be mentioned that, when a female tenant in tail dies without having barred the entail, a surviving husband can claim curtesy, on the usual conditions.[3] But upon the death of a male tenant in tail a surviving wife cannot claim dower.

In the above examples it has been assumed that the descent of the entail has not been restricted by the instrument creating it. A tail male cannot, of course, be inherited by a female descendant.

---

[3] See pp. 140, 141, *ante.*

The Modern Law

We may now consider the provisions of the Administration of Estates Act 1925. The first point to notice is that under these provisions the whole estate of the deceased is held upon a statutory trust to sell it, except that " personal chattels " (as defined by the Act) and reversionary (*i.e.* future) interests are not to be sold without special reason. Out of the proceeds of sale the deceased's personal representatives are to pay the funeral, testamentary and administration expenses and the deceased's debts. What is left over is called by the Act " the residuary estate," and it is this which goes to the statutory next of kin as defined by the Act.

(1) Surviving husband or wife

The rights of a surviving spouse must be met in full before other relatives can receive anything. The surviving spouse is entitled to:

(i) The " personal chattels " absolutely. These are defined in detail by the Act and include, broadly, all personal chattels not used for business purposes, but excluding money and securities for money.

(ii) A statutory legacy, free of death duties and costs, with interest at 4 per cent. per annum from the date of the death to the date of payment. If the deceased left surviving issue who attain a vested interest (under rules to be given hereafter), the amount of this legacy is £15,000; otherwise it is £40,000.[4]

(iii) An interest in one-half of the rest of the residuary estate. If the deceased left surviving issue who attain a vested interest, this interest is a life interest; otherwise it is an absolute interest, *i.e.* the spouse becomes absolute owner of that one-half of the rest of the residuary estate.

(iv) If the deceased left no surviving issue who attain a vested interest, no parent, no brother or sister of the whole blood, and no issue (who attain a vested interest) of a deceased brother or sister, the surviving spouse takes, not the limited interest described above, but the whole of the residuary estate absolutely.

(2) Surviving issue

Subject to the rights of any surviving spouse, the residuary estate goes to the surviving issue, if any, on the statutory trusts. These statutory trusts are as follows:

(a) *The per stirpes rule*

Issue of a child who has predeceased the intestate take between them the share that their deceased parent would have taken. Thus,

---

[4] The legacy was increased to these amounts by the Family Provision (Intestate Succession) Order 1972.

if the deceased has had two children, one of whom has predeceased the intestate leaving two children who have survived the intestate, then (subject to the next rule) the two children of the deceased child will take between them the one-half share that their deceased parent would have taken if he had survived the intestate.

(b) *The vesting rule*

No person attains a vested interest unless and until he attains the age of 18 [5] or marries under that age. Thus, if the intestate has had two children, both of whom survived the intestate, and one of these children attains 18 (or marries under that age), but the other dies under 18 without marrying, the child who attains 18 (or marries under that age) takes the entire residuary estate, subject to the rights of any surviving spouse.

In addition to these rules there are two *hotchpot rules* which apply to issue:

(c) *Inter vivos advancements*

If the deceased has made an *inter vivos* advancement to a *child* of the deceased, and that child claims a share of the estate on intestacy, he must bring into account the value of the advancement, unless the circumstances indicate a contrary intention on the part of the deceased. An advancement is a gift of property which is designed to set up, or advance, the child in life. The value of property which is to be brought into hotchpot under this rule is to be ascertained at the date of the deceased's death.

(d) *Gifts by will*

Where the deceased has died partially intestate, there is hotchpot under the rule given above and, in addition, any benefit conferred by the will upon a *child* or *remoter issue* of the deceased must be brought into hotchpot. This again is subject to any contrary intention that the deceased may have shown.

A simple illustration may be given of hotchpot under rule (c) above. Suppose that the deceased intestate has left two surviving children, C1 and C2, but no surviving spouse, and that during his lifetime the deceased made an *inter vivos* advancement of £1,000 to C1, and that the residuary estate is worth £5,000. If C1 wishes to claim a share of the residuary estate (as obviously he will on the facts given), he must bring the amount of his advancement into hotchpot. This makes the residuary estate worth £6,000, which is then divided equally between C1 and C2. C1, therefore, brings in £1,000 in order

---

[5] Family Law Reform Act 1969, s. 3. As regards the estate of an intestate dying before January 1, 1970, the relevant age was 21.

to take out £3,000. Needless to say, C1 is not, in fact, required to hand over a cheque for £1,000; the necessary calculation is made on paper and the actual residuary estate of £5,000 is distributed as to £2,000 to C1 and £3,000 to C2.

(3) Other relatives

The order of succession, if there are no surviving issue who attain a vested interest, is as follows:

(i) The deceased's parents absolutely—if more than one, in equal shares.

(ii) Brothers and sisters of the whole blood on the statutory trusts.

(iii) Brothers and sisters of the half blood on the statutory trusts.

(iv) Grandparents absolutely—if more than one, in equal shares.

(v) Uncles and aunts of the whole blood on the statutory trusts.

(vi) Uncles and aunts of the half blood on the statutory trusts.

If there are no relatives in the above list, the Crown or the Duchy of Lancaster or Cornwall is entitled to the residuary estate as *bona vacantia*. The Crown in its discretion may then make provision out of the estate for dependants of the deceased who are not amongst the statutory next of kin referred to above.

The " statutory trusts " mentioned above in relation to classes (ii), (iii), (v) and (vi) are the same as those for issue; but there are no hotchpot rules.

As already indicated,[6] relatives in classes (iii) to (vi) above cannot take if the deceased has left a surviving spouse, because in default of issue, parents, brothers and sisters of the whole blood and issue of a deceased brother or sister of the whole blood (taking under the *per stirpes* rule) the entire residuary estate goes to the surviving spouse absolutely.

Relatives in any given class take to the total exclusion of relatives in a lower class. If, for example, the deceased has left a surviving parent, no interest in the estate will be taken by brothers or sisters or by remoter relatives.

Special Rules Applicable to Spouses

(i) *Commorientes*

If there is no evidence as to whether the intestate survived his or her spouse, the intestate's estate is to be distributed on the basis that the spouse predeceased the intestate, so that effect is not given to the rights of a surviving spouse. This exception to the normal commorientes rule [7] applies only for the purposes of the law of intestacy and only as regards spouses.

---

[6] See p. 157, *ante*.
[7] See p. 149, *ante*.

(ii) *Redemption of life interest*

When a surviving spouse is entitled to a life interest under the law
of intestacy (*i.e.* when there are surviving issue), the spouse may elect
to take, instead of the life interest, a lump sum of money calculated
in accordance with provisions laid down in the Act. The right must
generally be exercised within 12 months of the first grant of repre-
sentation, but the court may extend the time on certain grounds.

(iii) *Option to purchase house*

A surviving spouse is given the right to purchase from the estate
at its true value any dwelling-house in which the surviving spouse
was resident at the date of the death of the deceased. There are
certain exceptions to the right, *e.g.* it does not apply where the house
is leasehold and the lease will come to an end within two years of the
death of the deceased or the landlord has the right to determine the
lease within that time. The right must be exercised within the same
time as the right mentioned in paragraph (ii) above, but here again
the court may extend the time on certain grounds.

(iv) *Hotchpot*

In cases of partial intestacy the amount of the statutory legacy
conferred upon the spouse (but not any other interest to which he or
she is entitled) must be diminished by the value of any benefit (other
than a specific bequest of personal chattels) conferred upon the spouse
by the will. There is no other hotchpot provision applicable to a spouse.

(v) *Separation*

If the parties are separated by judicial decree, the estate of the
intestate devolves as if the spouse were dead.[8]

Adopted children

For the purposes of an intestacy occurring on or after January 1,
1950, an adopted child ranks as a child of the adoptive parents, and
as not being a child of the natural parents. An adopted child is not,
however, entitled to inherit property under an entailed interest created
before the adoption order was made.

It may also be mentioned here that in any disposition made on or
after January 1, 1950, and after the adoption order in question, such
expressions as " child," " children " and " issue " include adopted
children, unless a contrary intention appears.[9]

---

[8] Matrimonial Causes Act 1973, s. 18 (2).
[9] Adoption Act 1958, ss. 16, 17, Sched. V, para. 4. For the purpose of the
Act, a disposition by will is "made" at the date of the testator's death if it
was executed, or confirmed by codicil, on or after April 1, 1959; otherwise it
is "made" at the date of the execution of the will.

Illegitimate children

In general illegitimate children had no rights under the law of intestacy,[10] and such expressions as " child " and " children " did not include illegitimate children, unless a contrary intention appeared. Now, however, by section 14 of the Family Law Reform Act 1969,[11] where either parent of an illegitimate child dies intestate, that child (or, if he is dead, his issue [12]) can take under the intestacy as if he had been legitimate; and if an illegitimate child dies intestate, each of his parents can take under the intestacy as if the child had been born legitimate.

---

[10] Under the Legitimacy Act 1926, s. 9, there was a limited exception applying as between an illegitimate child and his mother.

[11] Applying to deaths after 1969.

[12] *i.e.* legitimate issue: the Act does not generally abolish the distinction between legitimate and illegitimate birth for the purposes of intestacy.

APPENDIX

The Rent Act 1974

This Act received the Royal Assent on July 31, 1974, and came into force on August 14, 1974. Its effects may be summarised as follows:

(a) The protection of the main provisions of the Rent Act 1968 is extended to furnished tenancies (which previously enjoyed only the limited protection afforded by Part VI of that Act).

(b) The lettings to which Part VI of the 1968 Act applies are now limited to those (whether furnished or unfurnished) in respect of which the landlord resides on the same premises as the tenant.

(c) The rateable value limits for the purposes of Part VI of the 1968 Act are raised to £1,500 in Greater London and £750 elsewhere.

(d) Fixed-term lettings are no longer excluded from Part VI of the 1968 Act.

(e) To the list of tenancies excepted from the definition of " protected tenancy " under the 1968 Act are added lettings to students by specified educational institutions, and lettings for the purpose of a holiday.

INDEX

Easements—*cont.*
way, easement of, 91
Wheeldon v. *Burrows*, doctrine of, 86, 87
Entailed Interest. *See* Fee tail.
Entry, right of, 16, 31, 99
as legal interest, 16
Equity, 11 *et seq.*
equitable easement, 84
equitable estoppel, 13, 96
equitable interest, 12, 13, 14, 16
equitable lease, 27, 28
equitable mortgage, 107
of redemption. *See* Mortgages.
Escheat, 4
Estate, 4, 16
fee simple, 4
fee tail, 4, 5
freehold, 7
leasehold, 5
legal, 15, 16
life estate, 5
Estoppel, equitable, 13, 96
Estovers, 25
Executors, 140

Fee simple, 4, 7, 15, 17
words of limitation, 8, 9
Fee tail, 4, 21 *et seq.*
barring of, 21, 22, 61
devolution of, 63, 155, 156
special, 23
words of limitation, 8, 9, 10
Fines and recoveries, 21
Fishing rights, 20
Fixtures, 18, 19
Freehold,
estate, 7
tenure, 3

General words, 84

Heirs, 4, 8,. 155

Infants, 120, 121
Intestacy, 155 *et seq.*
adopted children, 160
canons of descent, common law, 4, 5, 63, 155, 156
commorientes, 159
dwelling-house, spouse's option to purchase, 160
hotchpot rules, 158, 159, 160
illegitimate children, 161
issue, rights of, 157, 158
per stirpes rule, 157, 158
personal chattels, 157, 160

Intestacy—*cont.*
redemption of spouse's life interest, 160
relatives entitled (other than issue), 159
spouse, rights of, 157, 159, 160
dwelling-house, option to purchase, 160
hotchpot, 160
redemption of life interest, 160
separation, judicial, 160
statutory trusts, 157
trust for sale, statutory, 157
vesting rule, 158

Joint tenancy. *See* Co-ownership.

Knight service, 3

Land charges. *See* Registration of charges.
Landlord and tenant. *See* Leaseholds.
Leaseholds, 5, 7, 27 *et seq.*
assignment, covenant against, 38, 39
covenants in leases (generally), 100, 101, 102
derogation from grant, 36
enfranchisement, 43, 44
enlargement of lease, 34, 35
equitable lease, 27, 28
essentials of lease, 27
forfeiture, 31 *et seq.*
bankruptcy of tenant, 33, 34
execution against lease, 33
mining leases, 33
relief against, 32
rent, non-payment of, for, 32
repairing covenant, breach of, for, 33
restrictions on, 32
sub-tenants, 34
waiver of, 31
future leases, 31
leases for lives, *etc.*, 30
legal estate, as, 15, 27
merger, 34
notice to quit, 29, 30
obligations of landlord and tenant, 35 *et seq.*
periodical tenancies, 28, 29, 30
perpetually renewable leases, 30
premises, condition of, 36, 37
quiet enjoyment, covenant for, 35
renewal of lease, contract for, 31
rent restriction. *See* security of tenure, *infra.*
repair, covenant to, 38